THE ANGEVINS AND THE CHARTER
(1154-1216)

LECTOR HOUSE PUBLIC DOMAIN WORKS

THE ANGEVINS AND THE CHARTER (1154-1216)

**STANLEY MEASE TOYNE,
SAMUEL EDWARD WINBOLT,
KENNETH NORMAN BELL**

ISBN: 978-93-5420-458-6

Published: 1913

LECTOR HOUSE LLP
E-MAIL: lectorpublishing@gmail.com

BELL'S ENGLISH HISTORY SOURCE BOOKS

THE ANGEVINS AND THE CHARTER
(1154-1216)

THE BEGINNING OF ENGLISH LAW, THE INVASION OF IRELAND AND THE CRUSADES

BY

S. M. TOYNE, M.A.

HEADMASTER OF ST. PETER'S SCHOOL, YORK
LATE ASSISTANT MASTER AT HAILEYBURY COLLEGE

GENERAL EDITORS:
S. E. WINBOLT, M.A., AND KENNETH BELL, M.A.

1913

CONTENTS

CONTENTS

ix

INTRODUCTION.

THIS series of English History Source Books is intended for use with any ordinary textbook of English History. Experience has conclusively shown that such apparatus is a valuable—nay, an indispensable—adjunct to the history lesson. It is capable of two main uses: either by way of lively illustration at the close of a lesson, or by way of inference-drawing, before the textbook is read, at the beginning of the lesson. The kind of problems and exercises that may be based on the documents are legion, and are admirably illustrated in a *History of England for Schools*, Part I., by Keatinge and Frazer, pp. 377-381. However, we have no wish to prescribe for the teacher the manner in which he shall exercise his craft, but simply to provide him and his pupils with materials hitherto not readily accessible for school purposes. The very moderate price of the books in this series should bring them within the reach of every secondary school. Source books enable the pupil to take a more active part than hitherto in the history lesson. Here is the apparatus, the raw material: its use we leave to teacher and taught.

Our belief is that the books may profitably be used by all grades of historical students between the standards of fourth-form boys in secondary schools and undergraduates at Universities. What differentiates students at one extreme from those at the other is not so much the kind of subject-matter dealt with, as the amount they can read into or extract from it.

In regard to choice of subject-matter, while trying to satisfy the natural demand for certain "stock" documents of vital importance, we hope to introduce much fresh and novel matter. It is our intention that the majority of the extracts should be lively in style—that is, personal, or descriptive, or rhetorical, or even strongly partisan—and should not so much profess to give the truth as supply data for inference. We aim at the greatest possible variety, and lay under contribution letters, biographies, ballads and poems, diaries, debates, and newspaper accounts. Economics, London, municipal, and social life generally, and local history, are represented in these pages.

The order of the extracts is strictly chronological, each being numbered, titled, and dated, and its authority given. The text is modernised, where necessary, to the extent of leaving no difficulties in reading.

We shall be most grateful to teachers and students who may send us suggestions for improvement.

S. E. Winbolt.
Kenneth Bell.

NOTE TO THIS VOLUME (1154-1216).

I have to acknowledge, with thanks to Messrs. Chatto & Windus, permission to reprint two extracts from Jocelin de Brakelond from their edition in the King's Classics; to the Clarendon Press, Oxford, permission to reprint passages from Mr. Orpen's translation of the *Song of Dermot*. The history of this period necessitates a rather large proportion of statutes, but the liveliness of style in the *Dialogus de Scaccario* and the interesting nature of its contents will, I hope, be considered to be sufficient excuse for the number of extracts from that one source.

S. M. T.

Haileybury, *January 1913*.

PART I.
STATUTES 1154-1216.

THE ANGEVINS AND THE CHARTER
(1154-1216)

CONSTITUTIONS OF CLARENDON, 1164.

Source. — *Historical Documents of the Middle Ages.* Henderson. Bohn's Libraries. G. Bell & Sons.

1. If a controversy concerning advowson and presentation of Churches arise between laymen, or between laymen and clerks, or between clerks, it shall be treated of and terminated in the court of the lord King.

3. Clerks charged and accused of anything, being summoned by the Justice of the King, shall come into his court, about to respond there for what it seems to the King's Court that he should respond there; and in the ecclesiastical court for what it seems he should respond there; so that the Justice of the King shall send to the Court of the Holy Church to see in what manner the affair will there be carried on. And if the clerk shall be convicted, or shall confess, the Church ought not to protect him further.

4. It is not lawful for his archbishops, bishops and persons of the kingdom to go out of the kingdom without the permission of the lord King. And if it please the King and they go out, they shall give assurance that neither in going, nor in making a stay, nor in returning, will they seek the hurt or harm of King or kingdom.

6. Laymen ought not to be accused unless through reliable and legal accusers and witnesses in the presence of the bishop, in such wise that the archdean do not lose his right nor anything which he ought to have from it.

7. No one who holds of the King in chief, and no one of his demesne servitors, shall be excommunicated, nor shall the lands of any one of them be placed under an interdict, unless first the lord King, if he be in the land, or his Justiciar, if he be without the kingdom, be asked to do justice concerning him.

9. If a quarrel arise between a clerk and a layman or between a layman and a clerk concerning any tenement which the clerk wishes to attach to the church property, but the layman to a lay fee: by the inquest of twelve lawful men, through the judgement of the Chief Justice of the King, it shall be determined in the presence of the Justice himself, whether the tenement belongs to the Church property or to the lay fee.

10. Whoever shall belong to the city or castle or fortress or demesne manor

of the lord King, if he be summoned by the archdean or bishop for any offence for which he ought to respond to them, and he be unwilling to answer their summonses, it is perfectly right to place him under the interdict: but he ought not to be excommunicated until the chief servitor of the lord King of that town shall be asked to compel him by law to answer the summonses.

12. When an archbishopric is vacant, or a bishopric, or an abbey, or a priory of the demesne of the King, it ought to be in his hand: and he ought to receive all the revenues and incomes from it, as demesne ones. And, when it comes to providing for the church, the lord King should summon the more important persons of the Church, and, in the lord King's own chapel, the election ought to take place with the assent of the lord King and with the counsel of the persons of the kingdom whom he had called for this purpose. And there, before he is consecrated, the person elected shall do homage and fealty to the lord King as to his liege lord, for his life and his members and his earthly honours, saving his order.

14. A church or cemetery shall not, contrary to the King's justice detain the chattels of those who are under penalty of forfeiture to the King, for they (the chattels) are the King's, whether they are found within the churches or without them.

16. The sons of rustics may not be ordained without the consent of the lord on whose land they are known to have been born.

ASSIZE OF CLARENDON, 1166.

Source.—MS. in Bodleian Library.

1. In the first place the aforesaid King Henry, by the counsel of all his barons, for the preservation of peace and the observing of justice, has decreed that an inquest shall be made throughout the separate counties, and throughout the separate hundreds, through twelve of the more lawful men of the hundred, and through four of the more lawful men of each township, upon oath that they will speak the truth: whether in their hundred or in their township there be any man who, since the lord King has been King, has been charged or published as being a robber or murderer or thief: or any one who is a harbourer of murderers or robbers or thieves. And the Justices shall make this inquest by themselves, and the Sheriffs by themselves.

2. And he who shall be found through the oath of the aforesaid persons to have been charged or published as being a robber or murderer or thief, or a receiver of them, since the lord King had been King, shall be taken and shall go to the ordeal of water, and shall swear that he was not a robber or murderer or thief or receiver of them since the lord King has been King, to the extent of five shillings as far as he knows.

3. And if the lord of him who has been taken, or his steward or his vassals, shall, as his sureties, demand him back within three days after he has been taken, he himself, and his chattels, shall be remanded under surety until he shall have done his law.

9. And let there be no one within his castle or without his castle, nor even in the honour of Wallingford, who shall forbid the sheriffs to enter into his court or his land to take the view of frank-pledge; and let all be under pledges; and let them be sent before the sheriffs under free pledge.

10. And in the cities or burghs, let no one have men or receive them in his home or his land or his soc, whom he will not take in hand to present before the Justice if they be required: or let them be in frank-pledge.

12. And if any one shall be taken who shall be possessed of robbed or stolen goods, if he be notorious and have evil testimony from the public, and have no warrant, he shall not have law. And if he be not notorious, on account of the goods in his possession, he shall go to the water.[1]

---

[1] THE JUDGMENT OF BOILING WATER.—"The priest shall sprinkle over them some of the water itself; and to those who are about to go into the judgement of God, to all of them, he shall give to drink of that same holy water. And when he shall have given it, moreover, he

14. The lord King wishes also that those who shall be tried and shall be absolved by the law if they be of very bad testimony and are publicly and disgracefully defamed by the testimony of many and public men, shall forswear the lands of the King, so that within eight days they shall cross the sea unless the wind detains them; and with the first wind which they shall have afterwards, they shall cross the sea; and they shall not return any more to England, unless by the mercy of the lord King: and there, and if they return, they shall be outlawed; and if they return they shall be taken as outlaws.

15. And the lord King forbids that any waif, that is vagabond or unknown person, shall be entertained anywhere except in the burgh, and there he shall not be entertained more than a night, unless he become ill there, or his horse, so that he can show an evident excuse.

20. The lord King forbids, moreover, that monks or canons or any religious house, receive any one of the petty people as monk or canon or brother, until they know of what testimony he is, unless he be sick unto death.

21. The lord King forbids, moreover, that any one in all England receive in his land or his soc or the house under him any one of that sect of renegades who were excommunicated and branded at Oxford. And if any one receive them, he himself shall be at the mercy of the lord King; and the house in which they have been shall be carried without the town and burned.

---

shall say to each one: 'I have given this water to thee or to you for a sign to-day.' Then pieces of wood shall be placed under the cauldron, and the priest shall say ... prayers when the water itself shall have begun to grow warm.—And he who puts his hand in the water for the trial itself, shall say the Lord's Prayer, and shall sign himself with the sign of the cross; and that boiling water shall hastily be put down near the fire, and the judge shall suspend that stone, bound to that measure, within that same water in the accustomed way: and thus he who enters to be tried by judgement shall extract it thence in the name of God himself. Afterwards with great diligence, his hand shall be thus wrapped up, signed with the seal of the judge, until the third day; when it shall be viewed and judged of by suitable men."—*Historical Documents of the Middle Ages*, p. 316. (Published by G. Bell & Sons.)

"THE KING'S OFFICERS AT FAULT."
THE INQUEST OF SHERIFFS, 1170.

Source.—MS. in Bodleian Library.

§ 5. Let an enquiry be made concerning the goods of those that fled on account of the Assize of Clarendon and of those that perished through that assize. Let it be known what was done and what left each hundred and vill and let it be written down exactly and in order. In like manner let an enquiry be made, whether any man was unjustly accused at that assize through bribery, malice, or any unjust cause.

§ 6. Let an enquiry be made concerning the aids for the marriage of the king's daughter. What left each hundred and vill, whether it be in revenue or pardons and to whom this money was given up and delivered.

§ 9. An enquiry shall be made, whether the sheriffs or any bailiffs whatsoever have returned anything of the goods they have taken and whether they have made their peace with men after they heard of the king's coming, in order to prevent a complaint coming from them to the lord king.

ASSIZE OF ARMS, 1181.

Source.—*Roger de Hoveden*, Vol. II., p. 261. Bohn's Libraries. G. Bell & Sons.

1. Whoever has a fiefdom of one knight, let him have a coat of mail, a helmet, a shield and a lance; and let every knight have as many coats of mail and helmets and shields and pikes as he has knights fiefdoms in his demesne.

3. Also let all burghers and the whole community of freemen have a doublet, an iron headpiece and a pike.

7. Let no Jew keep his coat of mail or his hauberk, but sell them or give them or get rid of them in some way, provided that they remain in the service of the King.

8. Let no man carry arms outside England except by order of the King.

THE SALADIN TITHE, 1188.

Source.—*Benedictus Abbas*, Vol. II., 31.

The King, on the advice of his faithful counsellors, chose clerks and laymen in whose wisdom he could confide and sent them through each county to collect the tenths according to the decree, which obtained in his land across the Channel. But from each town in the whole of England he had all the richer inhabitants chosen, for instance, from London 200 and from York 100 and from the other towns according to their number and wealth. All were ordered to present themselves to him on given days at given places. From these he took a tenth of their incomes and their real property. The valuation was effected by his officers, who had knowledge of their incomes and their goods. If he found any rebellious, he at once had them imprisoned and kept in chains until they had paid the uttermost farthing. He dealt in a similar manner with the Jews of his land, from whom he acquired an enormous sum of money.

THE LEVYING OF A FORCE, 1205.

**AN ATTEMPT TO BLEND THE FYRD OR "FOLKMOOT IN ARMS"
AND THE FEUDAL LEVY.**

Source.—*Patent Rolls*, I., 55.

The King to the Sheriff of Rutland greeting. It has been ordained with the assent of archbishops, bishops, counts, barons and all our loyal subjects of England, that throughout England nine fighting men shall find a tenth well equipped with horses and arms for the defence of our realm: that those nine provide for the tenth on a specified day two pounds towards his equipment. Furthermore we charge thee, as thou lovest thy goods and thyself, to provide that all the tenth men of thy district be at London for three weeks dating from Easter, being well equipped according as we have ordained.... It has been ordained also, that, if foreigners come to our shores, all shall attack them with one accord using force of arms. Let none make excuse or delay but go at the first rumour of the invasion.

JOHN'S CONCESSION OF ENGLAND TO THE POPE, 1213.

Source. — *Historical Documents of the Middle Ages.* Henderson. Bohn's Libraries. G. Bell & Sons.

John, by the grace of God, King of England, Lord of Ireland, Duke of Normandy and Aquitaine, Count of Anjou, to all the faithful of Christ who shall look upon this present Charter, greeting. We wish it to be known to all of you, through this our charter, furnished with our seal, that inasmuch as we had offended in many ways God and our mother the Holy Church, and in consequence are known to have very much needed the divine mercy, and cannot offer anything worthy for making due satisfaction to God and to the Church unless we humiliate ourselves and our kingdoms: we, wishing to humiliate ourselves for Him who humiliated Himself for us unto death, the Grace of the Holy Spirit inspiring, not induced by force or compelled by fear, but of our own good and spontaneous will, and by the common counsel of our barons, do offer and freely concede to God and His holy apostles Peter and Paul and to our mother the Holy Roman Church, and to our lord pope Innocent and to his Catholic successors, the whole kingdom of England and the whole kingdom of Ireland, with all their rights and appurtenances, for the remission of our own sins and of those of our whole race, as well for the living as for the dead; and now receiving and holding them, as it were a vassal, from God and the Roman Church, in the presence of that prudent man Gaudulph, subdeacon, and of the household of the lord pope, we perform and swear fealty for them to him our aforesaid lord pope Innocent and his Catholic successors and the Roman Church, according to the form appended; and in the presence of the lord pope, if we shall be able to come before him, we shall do liege homage to him; binding our successors and our heirs by our wife forever, in similar manner to perform fealty and show homage to him who shall be chief pontiff at that time, and to the Roman Church without demur. As a sign, moreover, of this our perpetual obligation and concession we will and establish that from the proper and especial revenues of our aforesaid kingdoms, for all the service and customs which we ought to render for them, saving in all things the penny of St. Peter, the Roman Church shall receive yearly a thousand marks sterling, namely at the feast of St. Michael five hundred marks, and at Easter five hundred marks — seven hundred, namely, for the kingdom of England, and three hundred for the kingdom of Ireland — saving to us and to our heirs our rights, liberties and regalia; all of which things, as they have been described above, we wish to have perpetually valid and firm; and we bind ourselves and our successors not to act counter to them. And if we or any one of our successors shall presume to attempt this,—whoever he be unless being duly warned he come to his senses, he shall lose his right to the kingdom, and this charter of our obligation and concession shall always remain firm.

FORM OF THE OATH OF FEALTY.

I, John, by the grace of God, King of England, and Lord of Ireland, from this hour forth will be faithful to God and St. Peter, and the Roman Church and my lord pope Innocent and his successors, who are ordained in a Catholic manner. I shall not bring it about by deed, word, consent or counsel, that they lose life or members or be taken captive. I will impede their being harmed, if I know of it, and will cause harm to be removed from them if I shall be able: otherwise, as quickly as I can I will intimate it or tell of it to such person as I believe for certain will inform them. Any counsel which they entrust to me through themselves or through their envoys or through their latters, I will keep secret, nor will I knowingly disclose it to any one to their harm. I will aid to the best of my ability in holding and defending against all men the patrimony of St. Peter, and especially the kingdom of England and the kingdom of Ireland. So may God and these Holy Gospels aid me.

SUMMONS TO A COUNCIL AT OXFORD, 1213.

Source.—*Report on the dignity of a Peer*, p. 2.

The King to the Sheriff of Oxford greeting. We charge thee to see that all the fighting men of thy bailliwick, who have been summoned, should come to us at Oxford with their arms for fifteen days from All Saints' Day: in like manner the barons, but without their arms: and see that four discreet men from thy county come to that same place for the same length of time to talk with us about the affairs of our realm. Given under my own hand.

MAGNA CHARTA, 1215.

Source.—*Historical Documents of the Middle Ages.* Henderson. Bohn's Libraries. G. Bell & Sons.

John, by the grace of God King of England, lord of Ireland, duke of Normandy and Aquitaine, count of Anjou: to the archbishops, bishops, abbots, earls, barons, justices, foresters, sheriffs, prevosts, serving men, and to all his bailiffs and faithful subjects, greeting. Know that we, by the will of God and for the safety of our soul, and of the souls of all our predecessors and our heirs, to the honour of God and for the exalting of the holy church and the bettering of our realm....

1. First of all have granted to God, and, for us and for our heirs forever, have confirmed, by this our present charter that the English Church shall be free and shall have its rights intact and its liberties uninfringed. And thus we will that it be observed.

As is apparent from the fact that we, spontaneously and of our own free will, before discord broke out between ourselves and our barons, did grant and by our charter confirm—and did cause the Lord Pope Innocent III. to confirm—freedom of elections, which is considered most important and most necessary to the Church of England. Which charter both we ourselves will observe, and we will that it be observed with good faith by our heirs forever. We have also granted to all freemen of our realm, on the part of ourselves and our heirs forever, all the subjoined liberties, to have and to hold, to them and to their heirs, from us and from our heirs:

2. If any one of our earls or barons, or of others holding from us in chief, through military service, shall die; and if, at the time of his death, his heir be of full age and owe a relief: he shall have his inheritance by paying the old relief; namely, the heir, or the heirs of an earl, by paying one hundred pounds for the whole barony of an earl; the heir or heirs of a baron, by paying one hundred pounds for the whole barony; the heir or heirs of a knight, by paying one hundred shillings at most for a whole knight's fee; and he who shall owe less shall give less, according to the ancient custom of fees.

3. But if the heir of any of the above persons shall be under age and in wardship,—when he comes of age, he shall have his inheritance without relief and without fine.

4. The administrator of the land of such heir who shall be under age shall take none but reasonable issues from the land of the heir, and reasonable customs and services; and this without destruction and waste of men or goods. And if we shall have committed the custody of any such land to the sheriff or to any other man

who ought to be responsible to us for the issues of it, and he cause destruction or waste to what is in his charge; we will fine him, and the land shall be handed over to two lawful and discreet men of that fee who shall answer to us, or to him to whom we shall have referred them, regarding those issues. And if we shall have given or sold to any one the custody of any such land, and he shall have caused destruction or waste to it,—he shall lose that custody, and it shall be given to two lawful and discreet men of that fee, who likewise shall answer to us, as has been explained.

5. The administrator, moreover, so long as he may have the custody of the land, shall keep in order from the issues of that land, the houses, parks, warrens, lakes, mills and other things pertaining to it. And he shall restore to the heir when he comes to full age, his whole land stocked with ploughs and wainnages, according as the time of the wainnage requires and the issues of the land will reasonably permit.

6. Heirs may marry without disparagement; so, nevertheless, that, before the marriage is contracted, it shall be announced to the relations by blood of the heir himself.

7. A widow, after the death of her husband, shall straightway and without difficulty, have her marriage portion and her inheritance, nor shall she give anything in return for her dowry, her marriage portion, or the inheritance which belonged to her, and which she and her husband held on the day of the death of that husband. And she may remain in the house of her husband, after his death for forty days: within which her dowry shall be paid over to her.

8. No widow shall be forced to marry when she prefers to live without a husband; so, however, that she gives security not to marry without our consent, if she hold from us, or the consent of the lord from whom she holds, if she hold from another.

9. Neither we nor our bailiffs shall seize any revenue for any debt, so long as the chattels of the debtor suffice to pay the debt; nor shall the sponsors of that debtor be distrained so long as that chief debtor has enough to pay the debt. But if the chief debtor fail in paying the debt, not having the wherewithal to pay it, the sponsors shall answer for the debt. And if they shall wish, they may have the lands and revenues of the debtor until satisfaction shall have been given them for the debt previously paid for him; unless the chief debtor shall show that he is quit in that respect towards those same sponsors.

10. If any one shall have taken any sum, great or small, as a loan from the Jews, and shall die before that debt is paid—that debt shall not bear interest so long as the heir, from whomever he may hold, shall be under age. And if the debt fall into our hands, we shall take nothing save the chattel contained in the deed.

11. And if any one dies owing a debt to the Jews, his wife shall have her dowry, and shall restore nothing of that debt. But if there shall remain not children of that dead man, and they shall be under age, the necessaries shall be provided for them according to the nature of the dead man's holding; and from the residue the debt shall be paid, saving the service due to the lords. In like manner shall be done

concerning debts that are due to others besides Jews.

12.[2] No scutage or aid shall be imposed in our realm unless by the common counsel of our realm; except for redeeming our body, and knighting our eldest son, and marrying once our eldest daughter. And for these purposes there shall only be given a reasonable aid. In like manner shall be done concerning the aids of the city of London.

13. And the city of London shall have all its old liberties and free customs as well by land as by water. Moreover, we will and grant that all other cities and burroughs, and towns and ports, shall have all their liberties and free customs.

14.[3] And in order to have the common counsel of the realm in the matter of assessing an aid otherwise than in the aforesaid cases, or of assessing a scutage,— we shall cause, under seal through our letters, the archbishops, bishops, abbots, earls, and greater barons to be summoned for a fixed day—for a term, namely, at least forty days distant—and for a fixed place. And, moreover, we shall cause to be summoned in general, through our sheriffs and bailiffs, all those who hold of us in chief. And in all those letters of summons we shall express the cause of the summons. And when a summons has thus been made, the business shall be proceeded with on the day appointed according to the counsel of those who shall be present, even though not all shall come who were summoned.

15.[4] We will not allow any one henceforth to take an aid from his freemen save for the redemption of his body, and the knighting of his eldest son, and the marrying, once, of his eldest daughter; and for these purposes there shall be given a reasonable aid only.

16. No one shall be forced to do more service for a knight's fee, or for another freeholding, than is due from it.

17. Common pleas shall not follow our court, but shall be held in a certain fixed place.

18. Assizes of novel disseisin, of mort d'ancestor, and of darrein presentment shall not be held save in their own counties, and in this way: we, or our chief justice, if we shall be absent from the kingdom, shall send two justices through each county four times a year; they, with four knights from each county, chosen by the county, shall hold the aforesaid assizes in the county, and on the day and at the place of the county court.

19. And if on the day of the county court the aforesaid assizes cannot be held, a sufficient number of knights and free tenants, from those who were present at the county court on that day, shall remain, so that through them the judgements may be suitably given, according as the matter may have been great or small.

20. A freeman shall only be amerced for a small offence according to the measure of that offence. And for a great offence he shall be amerced according to the

---

[2] These important articles were omitted in the charters sworn by subsequent kings.

[3] These important articles were omitted in the charters sworn by subsequent kings.

[4] These important articles were omitted in the charters sworn by subsequent kings.

magnitude of the offence, saving his contenement[5]; and a merchant, in the same way, saving his merchandise. And a villein, in the same way, if he fall under our mercy, shall be amerced saving his wainnage. And none of the aforesaid fines shall be imposed save upon oath of upright men from the neighbourhood.

21. Earls and barons shall not be amerced save through their peers, and only according to the measure of the offence.

22. No clerk shall be amerced for his lay tenement, except according to the manner of the other persons aforesaid; and not according to the amount of his ecclesiastical benefice.

23. Neither a town nor a man shall be forced to make bridges over the rivers, with the exception of those who, from of old and of right, ought to do it.

24. No sheriff, constable, coroners or other bailiffs of ours shall hold the pleas of our crown.

25. All counties, hundreds, wapentakes, and trithings—our demesne manors being excepted—shall continue according to the old farms, without any increase at all.

26. If any one holding from us a lay fee shall die, and our sheriff or bailiff can show our letters patent containing our summons for the debt which the dead man owed to us,—our sheriff or bailiff may be allowed to attach and enroll the chattels of the dead man to the value of that debt, through view of lawful men; in such way, however, that nothing shall be moved thence until the debt is paid which was plainly owed to us. And the residue shall be left to the executors that they may carry out the will of the dead man. And if nothing is owed to us by him, all the chattels shall go to the use prescribed by the deceased, saving their reasonable portions to his wife and children.

27. If any freeman shall have died intestate, his chattels shall be distributed through the hands of his near relatives and friends, by view of the church; saving to any one the debts which the dead man owed him.

28. No constable or other bailiff of ours shall take the corn or other chattels of any one except he straightway give money for them, or can be allowed a respite in that regard by the will of the seller.

29. No constable shall force any knight to pay money for castle-ward, if he be willing to perform that ward in person, or—he for a reasonable cause not being able to perform it himself—through another proper man. And if we shall have led or sent him on a military expedition, he shall be quit of ward according to the amount of time during which, through us, he shall have been in military service.

30. No sheriff nor bailiff of ours, nor any one else, shall take the horses or carts of any freeman for transport, unless by the will of that freeman.

31. Neither we nor our bailiffs shall take another's wood for castles or for other private uses, unless by the will of him to whom the wood belongs.

32. We shall not hold the lands of those convicted of felony longer than a year

---

[5] Means of subsistence.

and a day; and then the lands shall be restored to the lords of the fiefs.

33. Henceforth all the weirs in the Thames and Medway, and throughout all England, save on the sea-coast, shall be done away with entirely.

34. Henceforth the writ which is called "Praecipe" shall not be served on any one for any holding, so as to cause a free man to lose his court.

35. There shall be one measure of wine throughout our whole realm, and one measure of ale, and one measure of corn—namely, the London quart;—and one width of dyed and russet and hauberk cloths—namely, two ells below the selvage. And with weights, moreover, it shall be as with measures.

36. Henceforth nothing shall be given or taken for a writ of inquest in a matter concerning life or limb; but it shall be conceded gratis, and shall not be denied.

37. If any one hold from us in fee-farm or in socage, or in burkage, and hold land of another by military service, we shall not, by reason of that fee-farm, or socage, or burkage, have the wardship of his heir or of his land which is held in fee from another. Nor shall we have the wardship of that fee-farm, or socage, or burkage, unless that fee-farm owe military service. We shall not by reason of some petit-serjeantry which someone holds of us through the service of giving us knives or arrows or the like, have the wardship of his heir or of the land which he holds of another by military service.

38. No bailiff, on his own simple assertion, shall henceforth put any one to his law, without producing faithful witnesses in evidence.

39. No freeman shall be taken, or imprisoned, or disseized, or outlawed, or exiled, or in any way harmed—nor will we go upon or send upon him—save by the lawful judgement of his peers or by the law of the land.

40. To none will we sell, to none deny or delay, right or justice.

41. All merchants may safely and securely go out of England, and come into England, and delay and pass through England, as well by land as by water, for the purpose of buying and selling, free from all evil taxes, subject to the ancient and right customs—save in time of war, and if they are of the land at war against us. And if such be found in our land at the beginning of the war, they shall be held, without harm to their bodies and goods, until it shall be known to us or our chief justice how the merchants of our land are to be treated who shall, at that time be found in the land at war against us. And if ours shall be safe there, the others shall be safe in our land.

42. Henceforth, any person, saving his fealty to us, may go out of our realm and return to it, safely and securely, by land and by water, except, perhaps, for a brief period in time of war, for the common good of the realm. But prisoners and outlaws are excepted, according to the law of the realm; also people of a land at war against us, and the merchants, with regard to whom shall be done as we have said.

43. If anyone hold from any escheat—as from the honour of Wallingford, Nottingham, Boloin, Lancaster, or the other escheats which are in our hands and are

baronies—and shall die, his heir shall not give another relief, nor shall he perform for us other service than he would perform for a baron if that barony were in the hand of a baron; and we shall hold it in the same way in which the baron has held it.

44. Persons dwelling without the forest shall not henceforth come before the forest justices, through common summonses, unless they are impleaded or are the sponsors of some person or persons attached for matters concerning the forest.

45. We will not make men justices, constables, sheriffs, or bailiffs, unless they are such as know the law of the realm, and are minded to observe it rightly.

46. All barons who have founded abbeys for which they have charters of the Kings of England, or ancient right of tenure, shall have, as they ought to have, their custody when vacant.

47. All forests constituted as such in our time shall straightway be annulled; and the same shall be done for riverbanks which we closed[6] in our time.

[Here follow three temporary clauses.]

*   *   *   *   *

51. And straightway after peace is restored we shall remove from the realm all the foreign soldiers, cross-bowmen, servants, hirelings, who may have come with horses and arms to the harm of the realm.

52. If anyone shall have been disseized by us, or removed without a legal sentence of his peers, from his lands, castles, liberties or lawful right, we shall straightway restore them to him. And if a dispute shall arise concerning this matter it shall be settled according to the judgement of the twenty-five barons who are mentioned below as sureties for the peace. But with regard to all those things of which any one was, by King Henry our father, or King Richard our brother, disseized or dispossessed without legal judgement of his peers, which we have in our hand, or which others hold, and for which we ought to give a guarantee: we shall have respite until the common time for crusaders. Except with regard to those concerning which a plea was moved, or an inquest made by our order, before we took the cross. But when we return from our pilgrimage, or if, by chance, we desist from our pilgrimage, we shall straightway then show full justice regarding them.

53. We shall have the same respite, moreover, and in the same manner, in the matter of showing justice with regard to forests to be annulled and forests to remain, which Henry our father or Richard our brother constituted; and in the matter of wardships of lands which belong to the fee of another—wardships of which kind we have hitherto enjoyed by reason of the fee which some one held from us in military service: and in the matter of abbeys founded in the fee of another than

[6] The Latin is "quae per nos tempore nostro positae sunt in defenso." Henderson renders "made into places of defence." In Cassell's *Dict. of English History* it is rendered "in defiance." But *defensum* in Med. Latin = (1) "prohibition" hence the French *défense*, and (2) "a close season" for fishing or hunting. I suggest that here it is used in a sense midway between (1) and (2) and means "closed" permanently to the public, just as the forests were. Naturally there would be objections raised to new "close" forests and new "close" rivers. Both the other suggested translations appear meaningless.

ourselves—in which the lord of the fee may say that he has jurisdiction. And when we return, or if we desist from our pilgrimage, we shall straightway exhibit full justice to those complaining with regard to these matters.

*　　　　*　　　　*　　　　*　　　　*

60. Moreover, all the subjects of our realm, clergy as well as laity, shall, as far as pertains to them, observe, with regard to their vassals, all these aforesaid customs and liberties, which we have decreed shall, as far as pertains to us, be observed in our realm with regard to our own.

61. Inasmuch as, for the sake of God, and for the bettering of our realm, and for the more ready healing of the discord which has arisen between us and our barons, we have made all these aforesaid concessions—wishing them to enjoy for ever entire and firm stability, we make and grant to them the following security: that the barons, namely, may elect at their pleasure twenty-five barons from the realm, who ought, with all their strength, to observe, maintain and cause to be observed, the peace and privileges which we have granted to them and confirmed by this our present charter.

[Here follows "a treaty of peace" between John and the Barons.]

*　　　　*　　　　*　　　　*　　　　*

Moreover, it has been sworn on our part, as well as on the part of the barons, that all these above-mentioned provisions shall be observed with good faith and without evil intent. The witnesses being the above-mentioned and many others. Given through our hand in the plain called Runnimede between Windsor and Stanes, on the fifteenth day of June, in the seventeenth year of our reign.

EXTRACTS FROM THE DIALOGUS DE SCACCARIO, WRITTEN BY RICHARD FITZNEAL, BISHOP OF LONDON IN HENRY II. 'S REIGN:

Source. —*Historical Documents of the Middle Ages.* Henderson. Bohn's Libraries. G. Bell & Sons.

In the twenty-third year of the reign of King Henry II., while I was sitting at the window of a tower next to the river Thames, a man spoke to me impetuously, saying: "Master, hast thou not read that there is no use in science or in a treasure that is hidden?" When I replied to him, "I have read so," straightway he said: "Why, therefore, dost thou not teach others the knowledge concerning the exchequer which is said to be thine to such an extent, and commit it to writing lest it die with thee?"

*   *   *   *   *

1. WHAT THE EXCHEQUER IS, AND WHAT IS THE REASON OF THIS NAME.

Disciple. What is the exchequer?

Master. The exchequer is a quadrangular surface about ten feet in length, five in breadth, placed before those who sit around it in the manner of a table, and all around it, it has an edge about the height of one's four fingers, lest any thing placed upon it should fall off. There is placed over the top of the exchequer, moreover, a cloth bought at the Easter term, not an ordinary one, but a black one marked with stripes, the stripes being distant from each other the space of a foot or the breadth of a hand. In the spaces, moreover, are counters placed according to their values; about these we shall speak below. Although, moreover, such a surface is called exchequer, nevertheless this name is so changed about that the court itself, which sits when the exchequer does, is called exchequer: so that if at any time through a decree anything is established by common counsel, it is said to have been done at the exchequer of this or that year. As, moreover, one says to-day "at the exchequer," so one formerly said "at the tallies."

D. What is the reason of this name?

M. No truer one occurs to me at present than that it has a shape similar to that of a chess board.

D. Would the prudence of the ancients ever have called it so for its shape alone, when it might for a similar reason be called a table (tabularium)?

M. I was right in calling thee painstaking. There is another, but a more hidden reason. For just as, in a game of chess, there are certain grades of combatants and they proceed or stand still by certain laws or limitations, some presiding and others advancing: so, in this, some preside, some assist by reason of their office, and no one is free to exceed the fixed laws, as will be manifest from what is to follow. Moreover, as in chess, the battle is fought between Kings, so in this it is chiefly between two that the conflict takes place and the war is waged,—the treasurer, namely, and the sheriff who sits there to render account; the others sitting by as judges to see and to judge.

*   *   *   *   *

M. ... The barons, moreover, who sit at the exchequer shall pay nothing under the name of customs for the victuals of their household bought in the cities and burghs and ports. But if an officer of the revenues shall have compelled one of them to pay anything for these,—if only one of his servants is present who is willing to prove by taking an oath that the things have been bought for his master's use: to the baron indeed, the money exacted shall be restored entire, and the scoundrel of a collector shall pay a pecuniary punishment according to the quality of the person.

... If those who sit at the exchequer shall have mutually molested each other with any sort of contumelious attack, they shall make peace again; the others of their rank who serve with them acting as mediators, in such wise that satisfaction shall be rendered by him who, in their estimation, has injured an innocent person. But if he be unwilling to acquiesce, but rather persevere in his rashness, the matter shall be laid before the president, and afterwards, from him each one shall receive justice. But if, through the devil, the instigator of evil, who does not look with unmoved eyes on the joyous happiness of fraternal peace, it should happen that occasion for discord should come up among the greater officials themselves, and thence—which God forbid—a war of insults should arise; and, Satan adding goads, peace cannot be restored by the other colleagues in those labours:—the knowledge of all these things shall be reserved for the prince himself; who, according as God, in whose hand it is, inspires his heart, shall punish the offence; lest those who are set over others should seem to be able to do with impunity what they decree should be punished in others.

D. From this is manifest what Solomon says: "Death and life are in the power of the tongue," and likewise James: "The tongue is a little member and boasteth great things."

M. So it is; but let us proceed concerning the prerogatives. Common assessments are held at times, throughout the counties, by itinerant justices whom we call deambulatory or wandering judges; the assessments are called common because, when the sum is known which is required in common from those who have estates in the county, it is distributed according to the hides of land, so that when the time comes for payment at the exchequer, nothing of it is lacking. From all these payments all those who, by mandate of the King, sit at the Exchequer are entirely free, so that not only are none of them exacted from their domains, but also none from all their fiefs.

*　　　*　　　*　　　*　　　*

2. SCUTAGE AND MURDRUM.

D. Now if it please thee, do not delay to make clear what are scutage and murdrum....

M. It happens sometimes that, when the machinations of enemies threaten or attack the kingdom, the King decrees that, from the different Knights' fees, a certain sum shall be paid,—a mark, namely, or a pound; and from this come the payments or gifts to the soldiers. For the prince prefers to expose mercenaries, rather than natives, to the fortunes of war. And so this sum, which is paid in the name of the shields, is called scutage. From this, moreover, they who sit at the exchequer are quit.

Murder (murdrum), indeed, is properly called the secret death of somebody, whose slayer is not known. For "murdrum" means the same as "hidden" or "occult." Now in the primitive state of the kingdom after the conquest, those who were left of the Anglo-Saxon subjects secretly laid ambushes for the suspected and hated race of the Normans, and, here and there, when opportunity offered, killed them secretly in the woods and in remote places: when the Kings and their Ministers had for some years, with exquisite kinds of torture, raged against the Anglo-Saxons; and they, nevertheless, had not, in consequence of these measures altogether desisted—when he who had caused his death was not to be found, and it did not appear from his flight who he was. "As a vengeance it was decided that the hundred in which the dead Norman was found should be condemned to pay a large sum of tested silver to the treasury."

D. Ought not the occult death of an Anglo-Saxon like that of a Norman, to be reputed murder?

M. By the original institution it ought not to, as thou hast heard: but during the time that the English and Normans have now dwelt together, and mutually married and given in marriage, the nations have become so intermingled that one can hardly tell to-day—I speak of free men—who is of English and who of Norman race; excepting, however, the bondsmen who are called "villani," to whom it is not free, if their lords object, to depart from the condition of their station. On this account almost always when any one is found thus slain to-day, it is punished as murder; except in the case of those who show certain proofs, as we have said, of a servile condition.

3. THE FUSION OF ENGLISH AND NORMAN.

D. I wonder that this prince of singular excellence, and this man of most distinguished virtue, should have shown such mercy towards the race of the English, subjugated and suspected by him, that not only did he keep from harm the serfs by whom agriculture could be exercised, but left even to the nobles of the kingdom their estates and ample possessions.

M. Although these things do not pertain to the matters undertaken and concerning which I have bound myself, I will nevertheless freely expound what I have heard on these matters from the natives themselves. After the conquest of the kingdom, after the just overthrow of the rebels, when the King himself and the King's nobles went over the new places, a diligent inquiry was made as to who there were who, contending in war against the King, had saved themselves through flight. To all of these, and even to the heirs of those who had fallen in battle, all hope of the lands and estates and revenues which they had before possessed was precluded: for it was thought much for them even to enjoy the privilege of being alive under their enemies. But those who, having been called to the war, had not yet come together, or, occupied with family or any kind of necessary affairs had not been present,—when, in course of time, by their devoted service they had gained the favour of their lords, they began to have possessions for themselves alone; without hope of hereditary possession, but according to the pleasure of their lords. But as time went on, when, becoming hateful to their masters, they were here and there driven from their possessions, and there was no one to restore what had been taken away,—a common complaint of the natives came to the King to the effect that, thus hateful to all and despoiled of their property, they would be compelled to cross to foreign lands. Counsel at length having been taken on these matters, it was decided that what they, either on merits or having entered into a legal pact, had been able to obtain from their masters, should be conceded to them by inviolable right; but that, however, they should claim nothing for themselves by right of heredity from the time of the conquest of the race.

*   *   *   *   *

4. DANEGELD AND ESSARTS.

M. "Our island content with its own, does not need the goods of
    the stranger
    Therefore with every good right, our predecessors have
    called it,
    Truly the lap of riches; the home, too, of every delight."

On account of this she has suffered innumerable injuries from outsiders; for it is written "marked jewels attract the thief." For the robbers of the surrounding islands, making an irruption and depopulating the shores, carried off gold and silver and all sorts of precious things. But when the King and the natives, drawn up in warlike array, pressed on in defence of their race, they betook themselves to flight by sea. Now among these robbers almost the first, and always the most ready to do harm, was that warlike and numerous race of the Danes, who, besides possessing the common avarice of plunderers, pressed on the more eagerly because they claimed, of ancient right, some part in the domination of that kingdom, as the history of the Britons more fully relates. In order, therefore, to ward these off, it was decreed by the English Kings that, from each "hide" of the kingdom, by a certain perpetual right, two shillings of silver should be paid for the use of the brave men, who, patrolling and carefully watching the shores kept off the attack of the enemy. Therefore, since principally on account of the Danes this revenue was instituted, it is called "Danegeldum" or "Danegeldus." This, therefore, under the native kings, was paid yearly, as has been said, until the time of King William I. of the race and people of the Normans. For in his day the Danes as well as the other robbers by land and by sea, restrained their hostile attacks, knowing to be true that which is written, "When a strong man armed keepeth his palace his possessions are in peace." For they also knew, indeed, that men of surpassing valour do not suffer injuries to go unpunished. When, therefore, the land had long been quiet under the rule of this King, he became unwilling that that should be paid as a year-ly tax which had been exacted by the urgent necessity of a time of war, nor yet, however, on account of unforeseen cases, did he wish it to be entirely omitted. It was occasionally paid, therefore, in his time, and in that of his successor; that is, when from outside nations, wars or rumours of wars arose. But whenever it is paid, those who sit at the exchequer are free from it, as has been said. The sheriffs, too, although they are not counted under the barons of the exchequer, are quit of this for their domains, on account of the labour of collecting the tax. Know, more-over, that the domains of any one are called those which are cultivated at his own expense or labour, and likewise those which are possessed by his serfs in his name. For the serfs, according to the law of the kingdom, not only may be transferred by their lords from those places which they now possess and others; but they them-selves also are sold or sundered in every possible way; which right they them-selves, as well as the lands which they cultivate, in order to serve their masters, are considered domains. Likewise it is said by those to whom the ancient dignity of exchequer was known from what they had seen with their own eyes, that its bar-ons are free, for their domains, of essarts (clearance-fines) of the forests. With whom we also agree; adding the reservation, that they may be called quit of those essarts which had been made before the day on which the illustrious King Henry I. bade farewell to human affairs. For if they were quit of all, whenever made or to be made, the barons would seem to be free with impunity, according to their own will and judgment, to cut down their woods in which the Royal forest consists; which they can, in fact, by no means do with impunity, unless the consent of the King or of the chief forester has first been gained. Nay, those who have their domi-cile in the forest, may not take from their own woods what they want for the nec-essary uses of their homes, unless by view of those deputed to guard the forest. But there are many who wish to prove by their arguments that no one, by reason of his seat at the exchequer, is free from these essarts. If any one at all of those sit-ting there should, by any misfortune, commit a fault against the King, for which he would merit to be punished with a pecuniary fine, he would not be freed from that punishment except by special mandate of the King. Since, therefore, a clearance is a fault committed against the forest of the King, he who thus errs, and on this ac-count receives a penalty, ought not, as they say, to be acquitted unless by express mandate of the King. Now, although this reasoning is subtle and seems to some almost sufficient, it is to be said, in objection to it, that the penalty for clearance is fixed and common to those who err in this way; so that, namely, for the clearance of one acre of wheat land one shilling is paid; but for an acre in which oats are sown, six pence, by a perpetual law. Moreover, from these items a certain total sum arises, for which the sheriff is compelled to account to the exchequer; just as from the established two shillings or one from the different "hides" one sum arises which is called the common assessment. Since, therefore, in these respects, the essart has an express similitude with the common assessment, as has been said, it would seem as if the barons, not without justice, should be considered quit from the essarts, just as from the other common assessments. Likewise the authority, not to be despised, of custom and long usage is against them (the cavillers). For those whose memory is hoary call to mind that it was so in past times. I myself, who speak with thee, have, in modern times, looked upon Robert, Earl of Leicester, a discreet man learned in letters, and versed in matters of the law. He, while having an inborn virtue of mind, became also an emulator of his father's prudence: his industry examined into many matters under our Prince Henry the Second, whom neither fictitious prudence nor dissimulated folly deceives; so that, by the King's order, not only at the exchequer did Robert obtain the dignity of president, but also throughout the whole kingdom. He once, when the visitation of the forests, which they commonly call the "view," and which takes place every third year, was at hand, obtained a writ of the King to the effect that he should be quit of whatever might be demanded from his land for essarts, the sum being stated to which these amounted: and when this writ was brought and publicly read before the exchequer, all were amazed and wondered, saying, "does not this Earl invalidate our privileges?" And while those who sat there mutually regarded each other, Nigel, of blessed memory, the whilom Bishop of Ely, began speaking thus with modesty: "My lord earl, thou dost seem to have invalidated, by this writ, the prerogative of the exchequer, since thou hast obtained a mandate of the King for those things from which thou, by reason of thy seat at the exchequer, art free; and if one may logically draw an inference by deduction from the major term, whoever does not obtain a writ of the King concerning his essarts, will soon become answerable for their payment, but, with all due reverence, this mode of absolution is pernicious on account of the example it sets." When, therefore, as happens in doubtful cases, some were of one opinion, and others of another, there was brought in, as a valid argument in this matter, the yearly (pipe) roll of the time of that great King of whom we spoke above, under whom the dignity and the knowledge of the exchequer are said to have flourished in a high degree; and something was found which seemed to justify the bishop who made the assertion concerning the prerogative of those sitting there. Having heard these things, the earl, after deliberating a little with himself, said: "I confess that in this matter I obtained a writ of the King, not that I might invalidate your right, but that thus, without trouble, I might avoid the too unfortunate exaction—unknown, however, to the King—of the collectors." Abandoning his writ, therefore, he chose to be absolved on account of the prerogative of his seat. Some time after, when the aforesaid bishop, detained by infirmity, could not be present, and I myself supplied, as well as I could, his place at the exchequer, it happened that essarts were paid. When, therefore, what had been exacted from his domain had been paid, I complained publicly, alleging the right of exemption. By the common counsel and verdict of all, therefore, the sum which had already been paid was restored to me. Reserving therefore, what had been raised from his domain, I restored to his serfs, in its entirety, what had been exacted from each one, so that the memory might survive and be witness in this matter.

D. With all due reverence, one should not use examples, but reasons in these matters.

M. That is so; but it happens, at times, that the causes of things and the reasons of sayings are secret; and then it suffices to bring up examples relating to them; especially if they are taken from the cases of prudent men, whose deeds are circumspect and are not done without reason. But whatever we have said about these things taking part for this privilege or against it, thou may'st be sure that in this matter we have called nothing certain, unless what the authority of the King decreed should be observed. But the account of the forests and also the punishment or absolution of those who transgress with regard to them, whether it be a pecuniary or a corporal one, is kept separate from the other judgments of the kingdom, and is subjected to the will of the King alone or to that of some one of his intimates specially deputed for this purpose. It subsists by its own laws, which, they say, are not subject to the common law of the kingdom, but to the voluntary decree of the princes; so that whatever has been done according to its law may be said to be not absolutely just, but just according to the law of the forest. The forests, moreover, are the sanctuaries of the Kings and their greatest delight, thither they go for the sake of hunting, having laid aside their cares for a while, so that they may be refreshed by a short rest. There the serious, and at the same time the natural uproars of the court having ceased, they breathe in for a while the boon of pure liberty; whence it comes that they who transgress with regard to the forest are subject to the royal displeasure alone.

D. From my earliest youth I have learned that it is wrong for a prudent person to prefer to suffer ignorance rather than to demand the causes of things that have been said, in order, therefore, that the foregoing may more fully be made clear, do not put off revealing what a forest is.

*   *   *   *   *

5. THE FOREST.

M. The forest of the King is the safe dwelling-place of wild beasts; not of every kind, but of the kinds that live in woods; not in all places, but in fixed ones, and ones suitable for the purpose; whence it is called "foresta," the "e" being changed into "o," as if it were "feresta" —*i.e.* an abiding place for wild beasts.

D. Is there a forest of the King in each county?

M. No; but only of the wooded ones, where the wild beasts can have their lairs and ripe nourishment: nor does it matter to whom the woods belong, whether to the King or to the nobles of the kingdom,—the wild beasts can none the less run around everywhere free and unharmed.

*   *   *   *   *

6. THE SHERIFFS AND BAILIFFS.

M. All the sheriffs, therefore, and the bailiffs, to whom summonses are directed, are bound by the same necessity of the law; that is, by the authority of the royal mandate; that, namely, on the day mentioned and at the place designated, they shall come together and render satisfaction for their debts. In order that this may be clearer to thee, look more closely at the tenor of the summons itself, for it reads: "See to it, as thou dost love thyself and all thy belongings, that thou art at the exchequer of such and such a time and place; and that thou hast with thee whatever thou owest of the old farm and the new, and these debts written below." Pay attention, then, for two things are said which fit in with the two which follow: for this, "See to it as thou dost love thyself," refers to "that thou art there and there at such and such a time and place"; that expression, however, "and as thou dost love all thy belongings," seems to refer to this: "and that thou hast with thee these debts written below"; as if it were openly said, "thy absence, whoever thou art that receiveth a summons, unless it can be excused by causes necessary and defined by law, will redound to the peril of thy head; for thou wilt seem thus to have spurned the royal mandate, and to have acted irreverently in contempt of the royal majesty, if, being summoned concerning the matters for which thou art bounden to the King, thou dost neither come nor send one to excuse thee...."

*   *   *   *   *

7. LIVERIES.

D. What is that thou didst speak of as liveries of both kinds?

M. Some of the liveries are of poor people; as when, solely from the promptings of charity, one penny a day or two or more, are accorded to someone by the King for food and clothing. But some are of people who do service, so that they receive them as wages; such are the custodians of the palaces, the guardians of the royal temples, the pipers, the seizers of wolves, and the like. These, then, are liveries of different kinds which are paid for different reasons, but are counted among the fixed payments. And mark that, although the King is free to confer these liveries on any poor people whatever, they nevertheless, by ancient custom, are usually assigned to those who minister at court, and who, having no income, fall into bodily sickness and become unfit for labour.

PART II.
MISCELLANEOUS SOURCES.

HENRY PUTS HIS HOUSE IN ORDER, 1155-7.

Roger de Hoveden

Source.—*Roger de Hoveden*, Vol. I., Part II., pp. 255-6. Bohn's Libraries. G. Bell & Sons.

In the year 1155, being the first year of the reign of King Henry, son of the Empress Matilda, the said King laid siege to the castles of his enemies in England, and captured them; some of which he retained in his own hands, and some he levelled with the ground. After this, he crossed over into Normandy, and did homage to Louis, King of the Franks, for Normandy, Aquitaine, Anjou, Maine, and Touraine, with all their appurtenances.

In the year of grace 1156, being the second year of the reign of King Henry, son of the Empress Matilda, the said King returned from Normandy to England, and caused nearly all the castles, which had been erected in England in the time of King Stephen, to be demolished, and issued a new coinage, which was the only one received and current throughout the realm; he also established peace in the kingdom, and commanded the laws of King Henry, his grandfather, to be observed inviolably throughout the whole of his kingdom, and in many matters followed the advice of Theobald, Archbishop of Canterbury.

In the year of grace 1157, being the third year of the reign of King Henry, son of the Empress Matilda, the said King, by the advice and entreaty of Theobald, Archbishop of Canterbury, conferred the Chancellorship upon Thomas, Archdeacon of Canterbury, and bestowed upon him many revenues, both ecclesiastical and of a secular nature, and received him so much into his esteem and familiarity, that throughout the kingdom there was no one his equal, save the King alone.

In the same year, Malcolm, King of the Scots, came to the King of England at Chester, and did homage to him, in the same way that his grandfather had done homage to the former King Henry, saving always all his dignities.

SUPERSTITIONS AND CHARACTER OF THE IRISH, CIRC. 1155.

Giraldus Cambrensis

INSTANCE OF SUPERSTITION.

Source.—*Giraldus Cambrensis*, p. 79, Bohn's Libraries. G. Bell & Sons.

I now proceed to relate some wonderful occurrences which have happened within our times. About three years before the arrival of Earl John in Ireland, it chanced that a priest, who was journeying from Ulster towards Meath, was be-nighted in a certain wood on the borders of Meath. While, in company with only a young lad, he was watching by a fire which he had kindled under the branches of a spreading tree, lo! a wolf came up to them, and immediately addressed them to this effect: "Rest secure, and be not afraid, for there is no reason you should fear, where no fear is!" The travellers being struck with astonishment and alarm, the wolf added some orthodox words referring to God. The priest then implored him and adjured him by Almighty God and faith in the Trinity, not to hurt them, but to inform them what creature it was that in the shape of a beast uttered human words. The wolf, after giving catholic replies to all questions, added at last: "There are two of us, a man and a woman, natives of Ossory, who, through the curse of one Natalis, saint and abbot, are compelled every seven years to put off the human form, and depart from the dwellings of men. Quitting entirely the human form, we assume that of wolves. At the end of the seven years, if they chance to survive, two others being substituted in their places, they return to their country and their former shape. And now, she who is my partner in this visitation lies dangerously sick not far from hence, and, as she is at the point of death, I beseech you, inspired by divine charity, to give her the consolations of your priestly office."

At this word the priest followed the wolf trembling, as he led the way to a tree at no great distance, in the hollow of which he beheld a she-wolf, who under that shape was pouring forth human sighs and groans. On seeing the priest, having saluted him with human courtsey, she gave thanks to God, who in this extremity had vouchsafed to visit her with such consolation. She then received from the priest all the rites of the church, duly performed, as far as the last communion. This also she importunately demanded, earnestly supplicating him to complete his good offices by giving her the viaticum. The priest stoutly asserting that he was not provided with it, the he-wolf, who had withdrawn to a short distance, came back and pointed out a small missal-book, containing some consecrated wafers which the priest carried on his journey, suspended from his neck, under his garment, after the fashion of the country. He then intreated him not to deny them the gift of God, and the aid destined for them by Divine Providence; and to remove all doubt, using his claw for a hand, he tore off the skin of the she-wolf from the head down to the navel, folding it back. Thus she immediately presented the form of an old woman. The priest, seeing this, and compelled by his fear more than his reason, gave the communion; the recipient having earnestly implored it, and devoutly partaking of it. Immediately afterwards the he-wolf rolled back the skin, and fitted it to its original form.

THEIR CHARACTER.

Source.—*Giraldus Cambrensis*, p. 111. Bohn's Libraries. G. Bell & Sons.

It appears to me very remarkable, and deserving of notice, that, as in the present life the people of this nation are beyond all others, irascible and prompt to revenge, so also in the life that is after death, the saints of this country, exalted by their merits above those of other lands, appear to be of a vindictive temper. There appears to me no other way of accounting for this circumstance, but this: as the Irish people possessed no castles, while the country is full of marauders, who live by plunder, the people, and more especially the ecclesiastics, made it their practice to have recourse to the churches, instead of fortified places, as refuges for themselves and their property; and, by Divine Providence and permission, there was frequent need that the Church should visit her enemies with the severest chastisements; this being the only mode by which evildoers and impious men could be deterred from breaking the peace of ecclesiastical societies, and for securing even to a servile submission the reverence due to the very churches themselves, from a rude and irreligious people.

THE PAGANISM OF THE IRISH, CIRC. 1155.

Giraldus Cambrensis

Source.—*Giraldus Cambrensis*, p. 135. Bohn's Libraries. G. Bell & Sons.

They are given to treachery more than any other nation, and never keep the faith they have pledged, neither shame nor fear withholding them from constantly violating the most solemn obligations, which, when entered into with themselves, they are above all things anxious to have observed. So that, when you have used the utmost precaution, when you have been most vigilant for your own security and safety, by requiring oaths and hostages, by treaties of alliance firmly made, and by benefits of all kinds conferred, then begins your time to fear; for then especially their treachery is awake, when they suppose that, relying in the fulness of your security, you are off your guard. That is the moment for them to fly to their citadel of wickedness, turn against you their weapons of deceit, and endeavour to do you injury, by taking the opportunity of catching you unawares.

(G. C., p 138.)

There are some things which shame would prevent my relating, unless the course of my subject required it. For a filthy story seems to reflect a stain on the author, although it may display his skill. But the severity of history does not allow us either to sacrifice truth or affect modesty; and what is shameful in itself may be related by pure lips in decent words. There is then in the northern and most remote part of Ulster, namely, at Kenel Cunil, a nation which practices a most barbarous and abominable rite in creating their King. The whole people of that country being gathered in one place, a white mare is led into the midst of them, and he who is to be inaugurated, not as a prince, but as a brute, not as a king, but as an outlaw, comes before the people on all fours, confessing himself a beast with no less impudence than imprudence. The mare being immediately killed, and cut in pieces and boiled, a bath is prepared for him from the broth. Sitting in this he eats of the flesh which is brought to him, the people standing round and partaking of it also. He is also required to drink of the broth in which he is bathed, not drawing it in any vessel, nor even in his hand, but lapping it with his mouth. These unrighteous rites being duly accomplished, his royal authority and dominion are ratified.

(G. C., p. 139.)

Moreover, though the faith has been planted for so long a period in this country that it has grown to maturity, there are some corners of the land in which many are still unbaptised, and to whom, through the negligence of their pastors, the knowledge of the truth has never penetrated. I heard some sailors relate that, having been once driven by a violent storm, during Lent, to the northern islands and unexplored expanse of the sea of Connaught, they at last took shelter under a small island. Here they could hardly hold their ground by the help of their anchor, though they had three cables out or more. After three days, the storm abating, the sky becoming again clear, and the sea calm, they beheld at no great distance the features of a land which was before entirely unknown to them. From this land not long afterwards they saw a small boat rowing towards them. It was narrow and oblong, and made of wattled boughs, covered and sewn with the hides of beasts. In it were two men, stark naked, except that they wore broad belts of the skin of some animal fastened round their waists. They had long yellow hair, like the Irish, falling below the shoulders and covering great part of their bodies. The sailors finding that these men were from some part of Connaught, and spoke the Irish language, took them into the ship. All that they saw there was new to them and a subject of wonder. They said that they had never seen before a large ship, built of timber, or anything belonging to civilised man. Bread and cheese being offered to them, they refused to eat them, having no knowledge of either. Flesh, fish, and milk, they said, were their only food. Nor did they wear any clothes, except sometimes the skins of beasts, in cases of great necessity. Having inquired of the sailors whether they had on board any flesh with which they could satisfy their hunger, and being told in reply that it was not lawful to eat flesh during Lent, they were utterly ignorant what Lent was. Neither did they know anything about the year, the month, or the week; and by what names the days of the week were called was entirely beyond their conception. Being asked whether they were Christians, and had been baptised, they replied that to the present hour they had never heard of the name of Christ, and knew nothing about Him. On their return, they carried back a loaf and a cheese, that they might be able to astonish their countrymen by the sight of the provisions which the strangers ate.

It must be observed also, that the men who enjoy ecclesiastical immunity, and are called ecclesiastical men, although they be laics and have wives, and wear long hair hanging down below the shoulders, but only do not bear arms, wear for their protection, by authority of the Pope, fillets on the crown of their heads, as a mark of distinction. Moreover, these people, who have customs so very different from others, and so opposite to them, on making signs either with the hands or the head, beckon when they mean that you should go away, and nod backward as often as they wish to be rid of you. They are also prone to the failing of jealousy beyond any other nation. The women also, as well as the men, ride astride, with their legs stuck out on each side of the horse.

TRIBAL DISPUTE (1154-7).

Song of Dermot

Source.—*Song of Dermot.* Orpen. Clarendon Press. 1892.

l. 22.   Now in Leath-luinn there was a king,
O'Rourke he was called in Irish,
In Tisbrun, the barren, he dwelt,
A waste, a woody land.
But O'Rourke, the rich King,
Had a beautiful wife at this time,
The daughter of King Melaghlin
To whom Meath was subject.

*   *   *   *   *

l. 40.   Dermot, King of Leinster
Whom this lady loved so much,
Made pretence to her of loving,
While he did not love her at all,
But only wished to the utmost of his power
To avenge, if he could, the great shame
Which the men of Leath-luinn wrought of old
On the men of Leath-Mogha in his territory.
King Dermot often sent word
To the lady whom he so loved—
By letter and by messenger,
Often did the King send word
That she was altogether, in truth,
The thing in the world that he most loved;

l. 94.   King Dermot immediately
Came marching to the place
Where the lady had sent word
That she would be ready.
In this way Dermot the King
Carried off the lady at this time.

*   *   *   *   *

l. 110.   O'Rourke much grieving,
To Connaught went in all haste.

To the King of Connaught he relates all:

*   *   *   *   *

l. 126.   The King of Connaught sent word
To the King of Ossory in the first place,
That he should not fail their King
But should come to their aid.
And these men fully promised him
That they would make him
King in that territory
If they could cast out of it
King Dermot who was so bold.
And this man immediately revolted
Against his lord King Dermot;
And Melaghlin, the traitor,
Abandoned his lord;
And Mac Torkil of Dublin
Abandoned his lord at this moment.
There joined in the treason
Murrough O'Brien, an evil rebel.

*   *   *   *   *

l. 206.   When Dermot the King perceived
That he was betrayed at this time—
His own men failed him,
So completely was he betrayed—
And that they wished to take him
To hand him over and sell him to O'Rourke,
While the King of Connaught on the other hand
Should make a great destruction of him—
Why should I delay you
From your geste at all?
His people by the strong hand
Have cast out King Dermot,
Have wrested the whole kingdom from him
And have driven him from Ireland.
When the King was exiled
He took ship at Corkerau

.   .   .   .

His ships had a very fine breeze,
At Bristol they take the shore.

*   *   *   *   *

THE BULL OF POPE ADRIAN IV. EMPOWERING HENRY II. TO CONQUER IRELAND, A.D. 1155.

Source.—*Historical Documents of the Middle Ages*, p. 10. Henderson. Bohn's Libraries. G. Bell & Sons.

Bishop Adrian, servant of the servants of God, sends to his dearest son in Christ, the illustrious King of the English, greeting and apostolic benediction. Laudably and profitably enough thy magnificence thinks of extending thy glorious name on earth, and of heaping up rewards of eternal felicity in heaven, inasmuch as, like a good catholic prince, thou dost endeavour to enlarge the bounds of the Church, to declare the truth of the Christian faith to ignorant and barbarous nations, and to extirpate the plants of evil from the field of the Lord....

There is indeed no doubt, as thy Highness doth also acknowledge, that Ireland and all other islands which Christ the Sun of Righteousness has illumined, and which have received the doctrines of the Christian faith, belong to the jurisdiction of St. Peter and of the Holy Roman Church....

Thou hast signified to us, indeed, most beloved son in Christ, that thou dost desire to enter into the island of Ireland, in order to subject the people to the laws and to extirpate the vices that have there taken root, and that thou art willing to pay an annual pension to St. Peter of one penny from every house, and to preserve the rights of the churches in that land inviolate and entire....

[This bull was not thought to be genuine by the majority of historians, but Mr. Orpen in *Ireland under the Normans*, 1912, successfully proves its authenticity.]

THOMAS À BECKET. LIFE BEFORE HIS ELECTION (1155-1162).

Roger of Wendover

Source.—*Roger of Wendover, Annal 1162.* Bohn's Libraries. G. Bell & Sons.

The same year, the clergy and people of the whole province of Canterbury assembled at Westminster, where Thomas, the King's Chancellor, was solemnly elected, without opposition, to be Archbishop. This happened on Whitsunday: the Chancellor was ordained priest, by Walter Bishop of Rochester, in the church of Canterbury, and on the following Sunday was consecrated by Henry Bishop of Winchester, and solemnly enthroned. Messengers were immediately despatched to Rome, but they met the Pope on this side of the Alps entering France, and they returned to England, bringing with them the pall; which was placed on the altar in the Church of Canterbury. Thomas then, having taken the usual oaths, received the pall from the altar, and reverently put on him the robes of a high-priest. But this change of habit was preliminary to a change of heart also, for he now renounced secular cares, and attended only to the spiritual concerns of the Church and the gain of souls. He sent messengers to the King in Normandy, renouncing the Chancellorship and resigning the great seal. This act sank deep into the mind of the King, who looked upon himself alone as the cause of his resignation. This was the first occasion on which the King's feelings were ruffled towards Thomas Archbishop of Canterbury. Now this Thomas was a native of the City of London, and from his childhood was adorned with many virtues. From his birth, he used to take pleasure in invoking the blessed virgin, and, next to Christ, reposed all his hopes upon her. When he had finished his schooling, he entered the service of Theobald, Archbishop of Canterbury, and by his industry, soon won his way to intimacy and familiarity with him. Of his services and labours for the cause of God's Church, how he more than once visited the threshold of the apostles on matters of business, and how he successfully discharged his commissions, it is not easy to relate, seeing that his whole mind was devoted to examining and deciding causes and to instructing the people. He was first promoted by the Archbishop to be Archdeacon of Canterbury, and shortly after he was made King's Chancellor, in which capacity he wisely and prudently checked the rapacity of those kites, who, in servility to the King, had conspired to plunder the property both of the provincials and of the church.

DISPUTE CONCERNING CONSTITUTIONS OF CLARENDON (1164).

Roger de Hoveden

Source.—*Roger de Hoveden*, Vol. I., p. 259, *seqq.* Bohn's Libraries. G. Bell & Sons.

In the year of grace 1164, being the tenth year of the reign of King Henry, son of the Empress Matilda, the said Henry gave to Henry, duke of Saxony, his daughter Matilda in marriage. In the same year, having called together a great council, and all the archbishops and bishops of England being assembled in his presence, he requested them, out of their love for and obedience to him, and for the establishment of the kingdom, to receive the laws of King Henry, his grandfather, and faithfully to observe them: on which, Thomas, Archbishop of Canterbury, made answer for himself and the others, that they would receive those laws, which the King said were made by his grandfather, and with good faith would observe the same; saving their orders and the honour of God and of the Holy Church in all respects. But this reservation greatly displeased the King, and he used every possible method to make the bishops promise that they would, without any exception whatever, observe those laws; to this, however, the Archbishop of Canterbury would on no account agree.

After this, there came to England, a certain man belonging to the religious orders, named Philip de Eleemosyna being sent as a legate "a latere" by Alexander the supreme Pontiff, and all the cardinals, for the purpose of making peace between the King and the Archbishop of Canterbury; by whom the Pope and all the cardinals sent word to the Archbishop of Canterbury, that he must make peace with the King of England his master, and promise, without any exception, to obey his laws. Assenting, therefore, to this and other advice on the part of these great men, the Archbishop of Canterbury came to the King at Woodstock, and there made a promise to the King and agreed that he would, in good faith, and without any bad intent, observe his laws.

Shortly after this, the clergy and people of the kingdom being convened at Clarendon, the archbishop reported that he had made this concession to the King, and wishing to recede from his agreement, said that in making the concession he had greatly sinned, but would sin no longer in so doing. In consequence of this, the King's anger was greatly aroused against him, and he threatened him and his people with exile and death; upon which, the Bishops of Salisbury and Norwich came to the archbishop, together with Robert, Earl of Leicester, Reginald, Earl of Cornwall, and the two Templars, Richard de Hastings and Tostes de Saint Omer, and in tears threw themselves at the feet of archbishop, and begged that he would at least, for the sake of the King's dignity, come to him, and in the presence of the people, declare that he would observe his laws. The archbishop being consequently overcome by the entreaties of such great men, came to the King, and in the presence of the clergy, and the people, said that he acceded to those laws which the King called those of his grandfather. He also conceded that the bishops should receive those laws and promise to observe them. Upon this, the King gave orders to all the earls and barons of the realm, that they should go out and call to remembrance the laws of King Henry his grandfather, and reduce them to writing. When this had been done, the King commanded the archbishops and bishops to annex their seals to the said writing; but, while the others were ready so to do, the Archbishop of Canterbury swore that he would never annex his seal to that writing or confirm those laws.

When the King saw that he could not by these means attain his object, he ordered a written copy of these laws to be made, and gave a duplicate of it to the Archbishop of Canterbury, which he, in spite of the prohibition of the whole of the clergy, received from the King's hand, and turning to the clergy exclaimed "Courage brethren! by means of this writing we shall be enabled to discover the evil intentions of the King, and against whom we ought to be on our guard"; after which he retired from the court, and was unable by any means to recover the King's favour. And because he had acted inadvisedly in this matter, he suspended himself from the celebration of divine service from that hour, until such time as he himself, or his messenger, should have spoken thereon with our lord the Pope.

BECKET'S EXILE (1165).

Roger de Hoveden

Source.—*Roger de Hoveden*, Vol. I., pp. 266, 267. Bohn's Libraries. G. Bell & Sons.

At this moment the King sent him word by his knights to come to him without delay, and render to him a full account of all the receipts of the revenues of the kingdom during the time that he had been his Chancellor. And, in particular, he was questioned with reference to thirty thousand pounds of silver; on which the archbishop made answer: "My lord the King knows that I have often rendered him an account with reference to all the demands he is now making upon me before my election to the Archbishopric of Canterbury. But, upon my election to that See, the King's son, Henry, to whom the kingdom was bound by its oath, and all the barons of the exchequer, and Richard de Lucy, the justiciary of England, released me before God and the Holy Church, from all receipts and reckonings, and from all secular exactions on behalf of our lord the King, and thus, free and acquitted, was I elected to the administration of the duties of this office; and for that reason do I refuse to plead any further." The King, upon hearing this, said to his barons: "Make haste and pronounce judgment upon this person, who, being my liege-man, refuses to take his trial in my court"; on which they went forth and pronounced that he deserved to be arrested and placed in confinement. On hearing this, the King sent to him Reginald, Earl of Cornwall, and Robert, Earl of Leicester, to inform him of the judgment that had been pronounced upon him: who accordingly said to him: "Listen to the judgment pronounced upon you." To this, the bishop made answer: "In the name of Almighty God, and under penalty of excommunication, I forbid you this day to pronounce judgment upon me, inasmuch as I have appealed unto the presence of our lord the Pope." While the above-named earls were carrying this answer to the King, the archbishop went forth from the chamber, and going through the midst of them, reached his palfrey, and mounting it, left the palace, all the people shouting after him and saying: "Where are you going, traitor? Stop and hear your sentence!"

When, however, he had arrived at the outer gates, he found them shut, and was in great apprehension of being taken by his enemies, but Almighty God delivered him. For, Peter de Munctorio, one of his servants, espied a number of keys hanging on a nail near the gate, and taking them down, opened it, on which the archbishop sallied forth on horseback, the King's porters standing by, and uttering not a word. The archbishop made all haste to arrive at the house of some canons regular, where he was hospitably entertained, and commanded the tables to be set out and all the poor that were to be found before the gates to be introduced to eat and drink in the name of the Lord Jesus Christ. This was accordingly done; and he, together with them and his people, becomingly partook of the repast in the refectory of the canons, and, when it was finished, made his bed in the Church, between the nave and the altar. In the meantime, he had secretly ordered preparations to be made for his journey, as it was his intention to depart by night. At twilight, therefore, when the King and the rest were supping in the town, taking with him two friars of the Cistercian Order, the name of one of whom was Robert de Caune, and of the other, Scainen, and a single servant, who was called Roger de Broc, he went out of the town through the gate, which was left entirely without guards, and at daybreak arrived at Lincoln, and was entertained at the house of James. Here the archbishop changed his dress, and, changing his name, ordered himself to be called by that of Dereham; and being recognized by few persons, taking remote ways and bye-paths, he hastened towards the sea-shore, he and his attendants riding on at night, and concealing themselves in the day among his friends and acquaintances. At last they arrived at the sea-shore, and reaching the port of Sandwich, secretly embarked on board of a ship, and then, secretly setting sail, in the morning landed in Flanders, whence he immediately made his way to France.

Before, however, he had arrived at the court of Louis, King of the Franks, Gilbert Folliet, bishop of London, and William, Earl of Arundel, had arrived on behalf of the King of England, to prevent the King of France from receiving the Archbishop of Canterbury in his kingdom, and to request him to beg our lord the Pope, out of his love for him, not to receive the Archbishop of Canterbury into his favour. But the more pains the above-named envoys of the King of England took to have Archbishop of Canterbury expelled from the kingdom of France, the more did the King of France favour him and his cause.

THE RETURN (1170).

Roger de Hoveden

Source.—*Roger de Hoveden*, Vol. I., p. 330. Bohn's Libraries. G. Bell & Sons.

In the meantime, Louis, King of the Franks, and the archbishops, bishops, and nobles of the kingdom of France, besought the Roman Pontiff in behalf of the Archbishop of Canterbury, by the love which they bore him, and with protestations of implicit obedience, no longer to admit the excuses and delays which the King of England continually put forward, as he loved the kingdom of France and the honour of the Apostolic See. William, the bishop of Sens, also, being astonished at the desolate condition of the English Church, repaired to the Apostolic See, and obtained of the Roman Church, that, an end being put to all appeals, the King of the English should be subjected to excommunication, and his kingdom to interdict, unless peace were restored to the Church of Canterbury. Thus, at last, it pleased God, the dispenser of all things, to recompense the merits of His dearly beloved Thomas, and to crown his long labours with the victorious palm of martyrdom. He, therefore, brought the King of England to a better frame of mind, who, through the paternal exhortation of our lord the Pope, and by the advice of the King of the Franks, and of many bishops, received the archbishop again into favour, and allowed him to return to his church.

BECKET'S LIFE (1170).

Roger de Hoveden

Source.—*Roger de Hoveden*, Vol. I., p. 333. Bohn's Libraries. G. Bell & Sons.

As for his life, it was perfectly unimpeachable before God and man. To arise before daybreak did not seem to him a vain thing, as he knew that the Lord has promised a crown to the watchful. For every day he arose before daybreak, while all the rest were asleep, and entering his oratory would pray there for a long time; and then returning, he would awake his chaplains and clerks from their slumbers, and, the matins and the hours of the day being chaunted, devoutly celebrate the mass; and every day and night he received three or five flagellations from the hand of a priest. After the celebration of the mass, every day he re-entered his oratory, and, shutting the door after him, devoted himself to prayer with abundant tears; and no one but God alone knew the manner in which he afflicted his flesh. And thus did he do daily unto his flesh until the hour for dining, unless some unusual solemnity or remarkable cause prevented it. On coming forth from his oratory, he would come to dine among his people, not that he might sate his body with costly food, but that he might make his household cheerful thereby, and that he might fill the poor ones of the Lord with good things, whom, according to his means, he daily increased in numbers. And although costly and exquisite food and drink were set before him, still his only food and drink were bread and water.

One day, while the archbishop was sitting at the table of Alexander, the Supreme Pontiff, a person who was aware of this secret, placed before him a cup full of water. On the Supreme Pontiff taking it up, and tasting it, he found it to be the purest wine, and delicious to drink; on which he said: "I thought that this was water"; and on replacing the cup before the archbishop, the wine immediately returned to its former taste of water. Oh wondrous change by the right hand of the Most High!

Every day, when the archbishop arose from dinner, unless more important business prevented him, he always devoted himself to reading the Scriptures until the hour of vespers at the time of sunset. His bed was covered with soft coverlets and cloths of silk, embroidered on the surface with gold wrought therein; and while other persons were asleep, he alone used to lie on the bare floor before his bed, repeating psalms and hymns, and never ceasing from prayers, until at last, overcome with fatigue, he would gradually recline his head upon a stone, put beneath it in place of a pillow: and thus would his eyes enjoy sleep, while his heart was ever watchful for the Lord. His inner garment was of coarse sackcloth, made of goat's hair, with which his whole body was covered, from the arms down to the knees. But his outer garments were remarkable for their splendour and extreme costliness, to the end that, thus deceiving human eyes, he might please the sight of God. There was no individual acquainted with this secret of his way of living, with the exception of two—one of whom was Robert, Canon of Merton, his chaplain, and the name of the other was Brun, who had charge of his sackcloth garments, and washed them when necessary; and they were bound by their words and oaths that, during his life, they would disclose these facts to no one.

BECKET'S DEATH (1171).

Roger de Hoveden

Source.—*Roger de Hoveden*, Vol. I., pp. 335, 336. Bohn's Libraries. G. Bell & Sons.

Hardly had the father been residing one month in his see, when lo! on the fifth day of the feast of the Nativity of our Lord, there came to Canterbury four knights, or rather sworn satellites of Satan, whose names were as follows: William de Tracy, Hugh de Morville, Richard Briton, and Reginald Fitz-Urse, men of families remarkable for their respectability, but destined, by their daring to commit so enormous a crime, to blemish the glories of knighthood and the honours of their ancestors with perpetual ignominy. Accordingly, these persons made their way into the presence of the archbishop, and, as nothing salutary was the object of their message, in the malice they had conceived they omitted pronouncing any salutation, and addressed him in an insolent and haughty manner. Threats were exchanged on both sides and threat was answered with threat.

Now, the archbishop, with meekness and self-possession, had gone before them to the choir of the church, the monks having entreated, nay, forced him, on account of the solemnity of the season, to perform the service at vespers. When he perceived these armed men behind him, in the middle of the cloisters, it might have been expected that their own malignant feelings would have warned them to leave the church; but, neither did reverence for the solemn occasion dissuade them from their crime, nor the innocence of the patriarch prevent them from shedding his blood. Indeed, so entirely had their shameless determination to perpetrate the crime taken possession of them and blinded them, that they neither regarded the disgrace to their knighthood, nor took account of any danger. Therefore, following the archbishop with headlong and heedless steps, with drawn swords, they entered the church, and furiously cried aloud: "Where is this traitor?" After which, no one making answer, they repeated, "Where is the archbishop?" Upon this he, the confessor, and, shortly to be, the martyr in the cause of Christ, being sensible that under the first name he was falsely charged, and that, by virtue of his office, the other belonged to him, came down from the steps to meet them, and said: "Behold, here am I," showing such extraordinary presence of mind, that neither his mind seemed agitated by fear, nor his body by trepidation.

On this the knights instantly laid hands on him and seized him, that, for the perpetration of their design, they might drag him out of the church, but were unable so to do. The archbishop, on seeing his murderers with drawn swords, after the manner of one in prayer, bowed his head, uttering these as his last words: "To

God and to Saint Mary, and to the Saints, the patrons of this church, and to Saint Denis, I commend myself and the cause of the Church." After this, amid all these tortures, this martyr, with unconquerable spirit and admirable constancy, uttered not a word or cry, nor heaved a sigh, nor lifted his arm against the smiter; but, bowing his head, which he had exposed to their swords, held it unmoved until the deed was completed.

COMING OF DERMOT (1168-9).

Song of Dermot

Source.—*Song of Dermot.*

DERMOT HAD AN INTERVIEW WITH EARL RICHARD.

His daughter he offered him to wife,
The thing in the world that he most loved:
That he would let him have her to wife
And would give Leinster to him,
On condition that he would aid him
So that he should be able to subdue it.

EARL RICHARD (STRONGBOW) IN IRELAND, 1170.

Song of Dermot

l. 1501. Very soon afterwards Earl Richard
Landed at Waterford
Full fifteen hundred men he brought with him.

.   .   .   .   .

On St. Bartholomew's day
Earl Richard, the prudent,
Took by assault and won
The City of Waterford.

*   *   *   *   *

l. 1524. King Dermot speedily
Came there, be sure, right royally.
The King in his company
Brought there many of his barons,
And his daughter he brought there;
To the noble earl he gave her.
The earl honourably
Wedded her in the presence of the people.
King Dermot then gave
To the earl, who was so renowned,
Leinster he gave him
With his daughter, whom he so much loved,

Provided only that he should have the lordship
Of Leinster during his life.

.   .   .   .   .

Then they turned towards Dublin
The King and the renowned earl

*   *   *   *   *

l. 1644. Outside the walls of the city
Was the King encamped;

.   .   .   .   .

Now Dermot, the noble King,
Despatched Morice Regan,
And by Morice proclaimed
To the citizens of the city
That without delay, without any respite,
They should surrender without gainsaying.

.   .   .   .   .

And Miles the renowned baron
To the earl gave up the city.

.   .   .   .   .

And the King returned
To Ferns in his own country.

.   .   .   .   .

At Ferns then tarried
King Dermot during this winter.
The King, who was so noble,
Lies buried at Ferns.
King Dermot is dead.
May God have mercy on his soul.
All the Irish of the country
Revolted against the earl.

.   .   .   .   .

And the rich King of Connaught
Summoned to him
The Irish of all Ireland
In order to lay siege to Dublin.

*   *   *   *   *

l. 1767. The earl you must know, at this time
Was within the city, of a truth.
The son of Stephen promptly sent
Some of his men to the earl:
In order to aid and succour him
He sent men to him at this crisis,
When Robert had sent
About thirty-six of his men
To aid the earl Richard,

The traitors without any delay
Fell upon Robert,
In the town of Wexford
They wrongfully slew his men:

.   .   .   .

Within a castle on the Slaney ...
The traitors took Robert
And put him in prison in Begerin.

*   *   *   *   *

l. 2229. Earl Richard at this time
At Pembroke found the rich king.

.   .   .   .   .

The noble earl saluted him
In the name of the Son of the King of Majesty,
And the King graciously
Made answer to Earl Richard.
The King thereupon replied
"May God almighty bless you."

*   *   *   *   *

l. 2495. As soon as the King came to the sea
At Pembrokeshire, in order to cross over,
Lo! then at the harbour
Twelve traitors from Wexford
Came to land in a boat

.   .   .   .   .

"Hold it not, lord, as folly,"
Thus spake the traitors unto him,
"If we shall say to you—be it known to you all—
Why we have come to you.
We have taken yon rebellious vassal,
Robert Fitzstephen is his name,

.   .   .   .   .

In a strong prison we have placed him;
To thee we shall give him up, noble King,
Who art lord of the English,
And do you, noble renowned King,
Do your pleasure in this matter."
The King replied to them
"On this condition be ye welcome,
That ye hand over this man to me,
And then ye will see what I shall do with him."

HENRY II.'S INVASION OF IRELAND, 1171-2.

Song of Dermot

l. 2579. Hear, my lords, concerning King Henry,
          Who was the son of the empress,
          How he resolved to cross the sea
          And to conquer Ireland
          Entirely through the recommendation
          Of the noble earl, according to the people.
          King Henry then crossed over
          To Ireland with his ships.
          The King then brought with him
          Four hundred armed knights.
          King Henry when he took ship
          Put to sea at the Cross:
          At Pembrokeshire at this time
          The rich King put to sea.
          With him the noble earl crossed over,
          According to the statement of the old people.
          At Waterford the noble King
          Landed with four thousand English,
          On All Hallows' Day, of a truth,
          If the geste does not deceive us;
          Before the feast of St. Martin
          The King at length came to Ireland.
          With the King there crossed over
          Vassals of good kindred.

    *   *   *   *   *

l. 2614. The earl of his own free will
          Surrendered the city to the King:
          To the King he surrendered Waterford
          Of his own free will and agreement.
          Homage for Leinster
          He did to the King of England.

    *   *   *   *   *

          From Waterford King Henry
          Set out with his marquises,
          To Dublin with his men
          He went without delay.
          Richard, the noble and valiant earl,
          Straightway surrendered the city to him.
          Dublin King Henry gave
          To the custody of Hugh de Lacy
          And he afterwards guarded the city
          By the command of the King.
          And the King of England
          Thence turned towards Munster,
          To the City of Cashel

Went the King with his splendid following,
Where at that time was the seat
Of the archbishopric of Munster.
From Cashel the puissant King
Went on to Lismore.
King Henry Curt Mantel
At Lismore wished to fortify
A castle: so wished King Henry,
Who was the empress' son,
I know not why, but nevertheless
At this time, he put it off.
Towards Leinster the English King
Set out at this time:
Towards Leinster, the rich,
He went with his chivalry,
Eighteen weeks, nor more nor less,
According to what the old people say,
The duke of Normandy remained
In Ireland with his baronage.
Of Normandy at this time
The rich King was duke;
Of Gascony and of Brittany
Of Poitou, of Anjou, and of Maine,
Was King Henry called
Lord, according to the old people.
In Ireland was the King
About a fortnight and four months.
In the land up and down
Marched the noble King.

  .   .   .   .   .

While the renowned King
Was in the City of Dublin
Lo! a messenger in haste
... Came to announce to the King
That Henry his eldest son
Had in truth revolted against him,
And that he sought to deprive him wholly
Of the lordship of Normandy.

    *   *   *   *   *

l. 2763. And the King towards Normandy
Went with his great nobles
In order to make war against a son of his
Who wished to despoil him.
War had the rich King
With the French in Normandy.

In Ireland remained
The noble earl with his friends.

THE CONSTITUTIONS OF THE SYNOD OF CASHEL (1172).

Giraldus Cambrensis

Source.—*Giraldus Cambrensis*, p. 232. Bohn's Libraries. G. Bell & Sons.

First. It is decreed that all the faithful throughout Ireland shall eschew concubinage with their cousins and kinsfolk, and contract and adhere to lawful marriages.

Second. That children be catechised outside the church doors, and infants baptised at the consecrated fonts in the baptisteries of the churches.

Third. That all good Christians do pay the Tithes of beasts, corn and other produce, to the church of the parish of which they live.

Fourth. That all the lands and possessions of the church be entirely free from all exactions of secular men; and especially that neither the petty kings nor earls, or other great men in Ireland, nor their sons, nor any of their household, shall exact provisions and lodgings on any ecclesiastical territories, as the custom is, nor under any pretence presume to extort them by violent means; and that the detestable practice of extorting a loaf four times a year from the mills belonging to the churches, by neighbouring lords, shall henceforth be utterly abolished.

Fifth. That in the case of a homicide committed by laics, when it is compounded for by the adverse parties, none of the clergy, though of kindred to the perpetrators of the crime, shall contribute anything; that, as they were free from the guilt of the homicide, so they shall be also exonerated from any payment in satisfaction for it.

Sixth. That every good Christian, being sick and weak, shall solemnly make his last will and testament in the presence of his confessor and neighbours, and that, if he have any wife and children, all his moveable goods, his debts and servants' wages being first paid, shall be divided into three parts, one of which he shall bequeath to his children, another to his lawful wife, and the third to such uses as he shall declare. And if it shall happen that there be no lawful child or children, then his goods shall be equally divided between his wife and legatees. And if his wife die before him, then his goods shall be divided into two parts, of which the children shall take one, and his residuary legatees the other.

Seventh. That those who depart this life after a good confession shall be buried with masses and vigils and all due ceremonies.

Finally. That divine offices shall be henceforth celebrated in every part of Ireland, according to the forms and usages of the Church of England.

DISPUTES WITH HENRY'S SONS (1173).

Roger de Hoveden

Source.—*Roger de Hoveden*, Part 2, Vol. I., pp. 367 *seqq.* Bohn's Libraries. G. Bell & Sons.

There also came to Limoges the Earl of Maurienne, and desired to know how much of his own territory the King of England intended to grant to his son John; and on the King expressing an intention to give him the Castle of Chinon, the Castle of Lodun, and the Castle of Mirabel, the King, his son, would in nowise agree thereto, nor allow it to be done. For he was already greatly offended that his father was unwilling to assign to him some portion of his territories, where he, with his wife, might take up their residence. Indeed, he had requested his father to give him either Normandy, or Anjou, or England, which request he had made at the suggestion of the King of France, and of those of the Earls and Barons of England and Normandy, who disliked his father: and from this time it was that the King, the son, had been seeking pretexts and an opportunity for withdrawing from his father. And he had now so entirely revolted in feeling from obeying his wishes, that he could not even converse with him on any subject in a peaceable manner.

Having now gained his opportunity, both as to place and occasion, the King, the son, left his father, and proceeded to the King of France. However, Richard Barre, his chancellor, Walter, his chaplain, Ailward, his chamberlain, and William Blund, his apparitor, left him, and returned to the King, his father. Thus did the king's son lose both his feelings and his senses: he repulsed the innocent, persecuted a father, usurped authority, seized upon a kingdom; he alone was the guilty one, and yet a whole army conspired against his father. "So does the madness of one make many mad." For he it was who thirsted for the blood of a father, the gore of a parent!

In the meantime, Louis, King of the Franks, held a great council at Paris, at which he and all the principal men of France made oath to the son of the King of England that they would assist him in every way in expelling his father from the kingdom if he should not accede to his wishes: on which he swore to them that he would not make peace with his father, except with their sanction and consent. After this, he swore that he would give to Philip, Earl of Flanders, for his homage, a thousand pounds of yearly revenues in England, and the whole of Kent, together with Dover Castle, and Rochester Castle; to Matthew, Earl of Boulogne, for his homage, the Soke of Kirketon in Lindsey, and the earldom of Mortaigue, with the honour of Hay; and to Theobald, Earl of Blois, for his homage, two hundred pounds of yearly revenues in Anjou, and the Castle of Amboise, with all the jurisdiction which he had claimed to hold in Touraine; and he also quitted claim to him of all right that the King his father and himself had claimed in Chateau Regnaud. All these gifts, and many besides, that he had made to other persons, he confirmed under his new seal, which the King of France had ordered to be made for him.

Besides these, he made other gifts, which, under the same seal, he confirmed: namely, to William, King of Scotland, for his assistance, the whole of Northumberland as far as the river Tyne. To the brother of the same king, he gave, for his services, the Earldom of Huntingdon and of Cambridgeshire, and to Earl Hugh Bigot, for his services, the Castle of Norwich.

TROUBLE WITH SCOTLAND (1174).

Roger de Hoveden

Source.—*Roger de Hoveden*, Part 2, Vol. I., p. 377. Bohn's Libraries. G. Bell & Sons.

In the meantime, William, King of the Scots, came into Northumberland with a large force, and there with his Scotch and Galloway men committed execrable deeds. Infants, children, youths, aged men, all of both sexes, from the highest to the lowest, they slew alike without mercy or ransom. The priests and clergy they murdered in the very churches upon the altars. Consequently, wherever the Scots and the Galloway men came, horror and carnage prevailed. Shortly after, the King of the Scots sent his brother David to Leicester; but before he arrived there, Reginald, Earl of Cornwall, and Richard de Lacy, Justiciary of England, had burned the City of Leicester to the ground, together with its churches and buildings, with the exception of the castle.

THE PENANCE OF HENRY (1174).

Roger de Hoveden

Source.—*Roger de Hoveden*, Part 2, Vol. I., p. 383. Bohn's Libraries. G. Bell & Sons.

On the day after this, he[7] set out on a pilgrimage to the tomb of Saint Thomas the Martyr, Archbishop of Canterbury. On his approach, as soon as he was in sight of the church, in which the body of the blessed martyr lay buried, he dismounted from the horse on which he rode, took off his shoes, and, barefoot, clad in woollen garments, walked three miles to the tomb of the martyr, with such humility and compunction of heart, that it may be believed beyond a doubt to have been the work of Him who looketh down on the earth, and maketh it to tremble. To those who beheld them, his footsteps along the road on which he walked, seemed to be covered with blood, and really were so; for his tender feet being cut by the hard stones, a great quantity of blood flowed from them on to the ground. When he had arrived at the tomb, it was a holy thing to see the affliction which he suffered, with sobs and tears, and the discipline to which he submitted at the hands of the bishops and a great number of priests and monks. Here, also, aided by the prayers of many holy men, he passed the night, before the sepulchre of the blessed martyr, in prayer, fasting, and lamentations. As for the gifts and revenues, which, for the remission of his sins, he bestowed on this church, they can never under any circumstance be obliterated from the remembrance thereof. In the morning of the following day, after hearing mass, he departed thence, on the third day before the ides of July, being Saturday, with the intention of proceeding to London. And inasmuch as he was mindful of the Lord in his entire heart, the Lord granted unto him the victory over his enemies, and delivered them captive into his hands. For on the very same Saturday on which the King left Canterbury, William, King of the Scots, was taken prisoner at Alnwick by the above-named knights of Yorkshire, who pursued him after his retreat from Prudhoe. On the following day, namely on the seventh day before the calends of August, the King departed from Seleham, and proceeded to Northampton; on his arrival at which place, William, King of the Scots, was brought to him, with his feet fastened beneath a horse's belly.

---

[7] The King of England, the father.

END OF THE ECCLESIASTICAL DISPUTE (1175).

Roger de Hoveden

Source.—*Roger de Hoveden*, Part 2, Vol. I., p. 392. Bohn's Libraries. G. Bell & Sons.

"Those who are in holy orders are not allowed to give judgment on matters of life and death. Wherefore we do forbid them either themselves to take part in dismemberment, or to order it to be done by others. And if anyone shall be guilty of doing such a thing, let him be deprived of the office and position of the orders that have been granted to him. We do also forbid, under penalty of excommunication, any priest to hold the office of sheriff, or that of any secular public officer."

"Likewise, inasmuch as the church of God, according to the verity of the Gospel, ought to be the house of prayer, and not a den of thieves, and market for blood; under pain of excommunication we do forbid secular causes, in which the shedding of blood, or bodily punishment is likely to be the result, to be tried in churches or in churchyards. For it is absurd and cruel for judgment of bloodshed, to be discussed in the place which has also been appointed the place of refuge for the guilty."

THE ALBIGENSIAN HERESY IN TOULOUSE (1178).

Roger de Hoveden

Source.—*Roger de Hoveden*, Vol. I., pp. 471-475. Bohn's Libraries. G. Bell & Sons.

In the meantime the Arian heresy which, as previously mentioned, had been condemned in the province of Toulouse, had revived; and this coming to the ears of the King of France and the King of England, inflamed by zeal for the Christian faith, they determined personally to go thither, in order that they might entirely drive the before-named heretics from those parts. However, after a short time had intervened, it seemed to them that it might be more effectual if they sent thither wise men to convert the heretics to the Christian faith by their preaching and learning, than if they themselves were to hasten thither in person, for they were reminded of the words, "Tis enough to have commanded vengeance; more will the dread of your name effect than your sword; your presence diminishes your fame."

They therefore sent thither Peter, cardinal priest, titular of St. Chrysogonus, and legate of the Apostolic See, the Archbishops of Bourges and Narbonne, Reginald, Bishop of Bath, John, Bishop of Poitou, Henry, Abbot of Clairval, and many other ecclesiastics, in order that by their preaching they might convert the said heretics to the Christian faith, or on reasonable grounds prove them to be heretics, and separate them from the threshold of holy Mother Church and from communion with the faithful. In addition to this, the before-named Kings chose Raymond, Count of Toulouse, the Viscount of Touraine, Raymond of Neufchatel, and other influential men, and ordered them to act as assessors to the above-named cardinal and his associates in the faith of Christ, and to expel the said heretics from those parts by the power of their might. Accordingly, when the before-named cardinal and the other Catholic persons had entered Toulouse, they found there a certain wealthy man, who possessed two castles, one within the city and the other without the walls of the city, who, before their coming had confessed himself to be a sectary of the heretical corruption; and now, moved by terror, and desiring to screen this execrable sect, made pretence that he was a Christian. When the cardinal came to know this, he ordered the said wealthy person to be brought before him; on whose coming for the purpose of making confession of his faith, he was found to be in every article an antagonist of the Christian religion. Accordingly, he was pronounced by the aforesaid cardinal and the bishops who were with him, a manifest heretic, and condemned; and they gave orders that his property should be confiscated, and that the castles which he possessed, lofty and of great beauty, should be levelled with the ground. Upon seeing himself thus condemned, and his property confiscated, he came to the cardinal, and the bishops, his associates, and prostrating himself at their feet; asked pardon, and, penance being enjoined him, was led naked and scourged through the streets and lanes of the city. After this, he swore that he would go to Jerusalem, and remain there three years in the service of God, and if, after the said three years, he should return home, his possessions were to be restored to him on condition, however, that his castles should be levelled in testimony of his heretical depravity; he was also to give the count of Toulouse five hundred pounds of silver.

On these taking place, many of the heretics, fearing lest they might be dealt with in a similar manner, came to the cardinal and his associates, and secretly confessing their errors and asking pardon, obtained mercy. In the meanwhile, it came to their ears, that certain false brethren, namely Raymond, Bernard, the son of Raymond, and certain other heresiarchs, transforming themselves into angels of light, while they were those of Satan, and preaching what was contrary to the Christian faith, led astray the minds of many by their false preaching, and had dragged them with themselves to hell. These being summoned to come into the presence of the cardinal and his associates, for the purpose of making confession of their faith, made answer that they would come before them if they should have a safe conduct in going and returning. A safe conduct, in going and returning, being accordingly given to them, they came before the above-named cardinal and the bishops, barons, clergy, and people who were present, and produced before them a certain paper in which they had written down the articles of their faith. On their reading this at length, there seemed in it certain expressions of a suspicious nature, which, unless more fully expressed, might possibly conceal the heresy which they preached. When one of them attempted to explain the articles so written, and to speak in Latin, he was barely able to connect two words, being utterly ignorant of the Latin language. Upon this it was necessary for the cardinal and the bishops to bring themselves more on a level with them, and, in consequence of their ignorance, to use the vulgar tongue. Accordingly, on being examined as to the articles of the Christian faith, they made answer as to all the articles of the faith as soundly and as circumspectly as if they had been most sincere Christians.

Upon the Count of Toulouse and others, who had formerly heard them preach what was contrary to the Christian faith, hearing this statement from them, being struck with the greatest astonishment, and inflamed with zeal for the Christian faith, they arose and most clearly convicted them to their faces of having lied; saying that they had heard from some of them that there were two Gods, the one good and the other bad, the good one having only made things invisible and which cannot be changed or corrupted, the bad one, the heavens, the earth, man and the other things visible. Others again affirmed that they had heard at their preaching, that the body of Christ was not made by the administration of a priest who was unworthy, or who had been convicted of any crime. Others again said that they had heard from them that baptism was of no use to infants, and the utterance of numerous other blasphemies against God and the Holy Church, and the Catholic faith, which, by reason of their abominable enormity, it is better to be silent upon than to disclose. The heretics, however, contradicted these matters, and said that they had given false testimony against them. For they said publicly, in presence of the before-named cardinal and bishops, and all the people there present, and made confession, and stoutly asserted, that there is but one God most high, who has made all things visible and invisible, and entirely denied that there were two first principles of things. They also confessed that the priest, whether good or bad, whether just or unjust, and whether such a character that they knew him beyond doubt to be an adulterer or criminal in other respects, was able to make the body and blood of Christ, and that, through the ministration of a priest of this character, and by virtue of the divine words which were pronounced by the Lord, bread and wine were really changed in substance into the body and blood of Christ. When, however, they had been convicted by many and competent witnesses, and many persons were still preparing to bear witness against them, because the Church is not wont to deny the bosom of mercy to those who turn thereto, they carefully warned them, laying aside all heretical corruptions, to return to the unity of the faith. They also advised them, as they had been excommunicated by our Lord, the Pope, and the before-named cardinal, and the Archbishops of Bourges and Narbonne, and the Bishop of Toulouse, on account of their perverse preaching and schism, to come to be reconciled to the Catholic faith, according to the forms prescribed by the Church. This, however, being warped into tortuous ways, and hardened by abandoned habits, they refused to do, on which the said cardinal, and the above-mentioned Bishops, together with the before-named Bishop of Poitiers, and the other religious men who had assisted them throughout, in the sight of the whole people, with lighted candles again denounced them as excommunicated, and condemned them, together with their prompter, the devil, and gave orders to all the faithful in Christ, thenceforth cautiously to avoid the before-named Raymond and Bernard, and their accomplices, as persons excommunicated and handed over to Satan; and that if at any time in future they should preach to them anything else than what they had confessed in their hearing, they should reject their preaching as false, and contrary to the Catholic and Apostolic faith, and drive them as heretics and forerunners of Anti-Christ to a distance from their territories. Moreover, the Count of Toulouse, and the other more influential men of the province, in presence of all the people gave assurance on oath, that from that time forward they would neither, for entreaty nor for money, support the heretics.

THE ELECTION OF AN ABBOT (1182).

Jocelin de Brakelond

Source.—*Jocelin de Brakelond*, Chapter 2. King's Classics. Chatto & Windus.

At last the prior and the twelve that were with him, after many fatigues and delays, stood before the King at Waltham, the manor of the Bishop of Winchester, upon the second Sunday in Lent. The King graciously received them; and, saying that he wished to act in accordance with the will of God and the honour of our Church, commanded the brethren by prolocutors—namely, Richard, the Bishop of Winchester, and Geoffrey, the chancellor, afterwards Archbishop of York—that they should nominate three members of our convent. The prior and brethren retiring as if to confer thereupon,—drew forth the sealed writing and opened it, and found the names written in this order—Samson, sub-sacrista; Roger, celerarius; Hugh, tercius prior. Hereupon those brethren who were of higher standing blushed with shame; they also marvelled that this same Hugh should be at once elector and elected. But, inasmuch as they could not alter what was done, by mutual arrangement they changed the order of the names; first naming Hugh, because he was third prior; secondly, Roger the cellarer; thirdly, Samson, thus literally making the last first, and the first last. The King, first enquiring whether they were born in his realm, and in whose lordship, said he knew them not, directing that with those three, some other three of the convent should be nominated. This being assented to, William the Sacrist said, "Our prior ought to be nominated because he is our head," which was directly allowed. The prior said, "William the Sacrist is a good man"; the like was said of Dennis, and that was settled. These being nominated before the King without any delay, the King marvelled, saying, "These men have been speedy in their work; God is with them."

Next the King commanded that, for the honour of his kingdom, they should name three persons of other houses. On hearing this, the brethren were afraid, suspecting some craft. At last, upon conference, it was resolved that they should name three, but upon this understanding, that they would not receive any one of those three, unless by assent of the convent at home. And they named these three— Master Nicholas of Waringford, afterwards (for a season) Abbot of Malmesbury; Bertrand, Prior of St. Faith's, afterwards Abbot of Chertsey; and Master H. of St. Neot's, a monk of Bec, a man highly religious, and very circumspect in spiritual as well as temporal affairs.

This being done, the King thanked them, and ordered that three should be struck off of the nine; and forthwith the three strangers were struck off, namely, the Prior of St. Faith's, afterwards Abbot of Chertsey, Nicholas, a monk of St. Albans, afterwards Abbot of Malmesbury, and the Prior of St. Neot's. William the Sacrist voluntarily retired, two of the five were struck out by command of the King, and, ultimately, one out of the remaining three. There then remained but two, the Prior and Samson. Then at length the before-named prolocutors of our lord the King were called to the council of the brethren: and Dennis, speaking as one for all began by commending the persons of the prior and Samson, saying, that each of them was learned, each was good, each was of meritorious life and good character. But always in the corner of his discourse he gave prominence to Samson, multiplying words in his praise, saying that he was a man strict in life, severe in reforming excesses, and ready to work hard; heedful, moreover, in secular matters, and approved in various offices. The Bishop of Winchester replied, "We see what it is you wish to say; from your address we gather that your prior seems to you, to have been somewhat remiss, and that, in fact, you wish to have him who is called Samson." Dennis answered, "Either of them is good, but, by God's help, we desire to have the best." To whom the bishop, "Of two good men the better should be chosen. Speak out at once; is it your wish to have Samson?" Whereupon several, in fact the majority, answered clearly, "We do wish Samson." No one gainsaid this, though some studiously held their peace, being fearful of offending either one or the other.

Samson was then named to the King, and after a brief consultation with those about him, the King called all in, and said, "You present to me Samson—I know him not; had you presented to me your prior, I should have accepted him, because I know and am well acquainted with him; but now I will do as you desire me. Take heed to yourselves; by the very eyes of God, if you have done ill, I shall call you to severe account." And he inquired of the prior, whether he assented to this choice and agreed thereto; who replied that he was well content it should be so, and that Samson was worthy of a much greater dignity. Then the elect, falling down at the King's feet and kissing them, hastily arose, and forthwith went towards the altar, erect in gait, and with unmoved countenance, singing "Miserere mei Deus" together with his brethren. The King, observing this, said to the bystanders, "By the eyes of God, this abbot-elect thinks himself worthy to govern an abbey!"

JOHN IN IRELAND (1185).

Giraldus Cambrensis

Source.—*Giraldus Cambrensis*, p. 309. Bohn's Libraries. G. Bell & Sons.

All things necessary for this great expedition having been prepared and made ready by the royal commands, John, the King of England's youngest son, on whom the dominion of Ireland had been lately conferred, took his journey by the coast road of South Wales towards Menevia and arrived at Pembroke. He was accompanied by a person of the highest station, Ranulf de Glanville, the King's chief privy counsellor and Justiciary of all England, who conducted him on board ship. On Wednesday, in Easter week, the breeze blowing favourably from the eastward, he embarked in the noble fleet which lay at anchor in Milford harbour, and on account of the sudden change of wind was prevented visiting the venerable church of St. David's, an unpropitious omen. Setting sail the same evening, the fleet accomplished its passage and reached the port of Waterford about noon on the day following, having on board about three hundred men-at-arms, and a large force of horse soldiers and archers.

*　　　*　　　*　　　*　　　*

I think it, therefore, not amiss that I should briefly state why, and from what causes, this first enterprise of the King's son did not fulfil his expectations; the success not being equal to the vast preparations for it.... I should say, then, that the first and principal cause of these mischances, was the King's not having listened to the solemn call of the patriarch Heraclius, before mentioned, and either gone himself, or at least sent one of his sons on his behalf, with ready devotion, in obedience to the commands of Christ. But instead of this, at the moment of this memorable summons, and in the very presence of the venerable envoy charged with it, he sent this son of his, with a retinue and outfit more sumptuous than profitable, not to the East, but to the West, not against the Saracens, but against Christians; for his own aggrandisement, not for the cause of Jesus Christ.

Another cause was this; as soon as the King's son landed in Ireland, there met him at Waterford a great many of the Irish of the better class in those parts; men who, having been hitherto loyal to the English and disposed to be peaceable, came to congratulate him as their new lord, and receive him with the kiss of peace. But our newcomers and Normans not only treated them with contempt and derision, but even rudely pulled them by their beards, which the Irishmen wore full and long, according to the custom of their country. No sooner, however, had they made their escape, than they withdrew from the neighbourhood with all their households, and, betaking themselves to the King of Limerick, the prince of Cork, and Roderick, King of Connaught, gave full particulars of all that they had observed during their visit to the King's son. They said that they found him to be a mere boy, surrounded by others almost as young as himself; and that the young prince abandoned himself to juvenile pursuits; and they further declared, that what they saw promised no mature or stable counsels, no security for the peace of Ireland.

On hearing this, the princes of Limerick, Connaught and Cork, who were at that time the mainstay of Ireland, although they were prepared to wait upon the young King's son and offer him their homage and submission with the usual forms, began to consider among themselves to what greater evils these small beginnings might lead, and what course would be taken with the proud and independent, when good and peaceable subjects were thus treated. They then resolved unanimously to resist the English, and defend with their lives their ancient liberties; and the better to carry this resolution into effect, a new league was generally entered into, and those who were before enemies were now reconciled, and became friends....

Another cause is this: We took away their lands from our own Irishmen, who had faithfully stood by us from the first coming over of Fitz-Stephen and the earl, and have given them to our newcomers. These Irish, therefore, betaking themselves to our enemies, became spies upon us, and guides to shew them the way to us, having the more power to do us injury from their former familiarity with us. Besides, the care and custody of all the towns and castles on the sea-coast, with the lands, revenues and tributes appertaining to them, which ought to have been administered for the public good and for defence against the enemy, were assigned to persons who thought only of hunting-out money; and keeping themselves carefully within the town walls, they spent their time and all that they had in drunkenness and surfeiting, to the loss and damage of the good citizens, instead of the annoyance of the enemy....

In the meantime this was the state of the island: all the roads were impracticable, all communications cut off; no security anywhere from the broad axes of the Irish; new reports daily of fresh losses by the English. Such was the condition of the country outside the towns. Within the walls, there was some semblance of order and tranquillity; and with plenty of wine and money, delinquencies in all quarters were easily atoned. Besides, when the storm was gathering in the enemy's quarters, it was time for the troops to look at their arms, instead of being immersed in civil affairs. But instead of this, there was so much vexatious litigation, that the veteran soldiers were more harassed by their adversaries within, than by the enemy without the walls....

I must add to my account of the mischiefs done by the new Government, one that is the greatest of all. Not only do we neglect to make any offering to the Church of Christ, not only are the honours and thanks due to God unacknowledged by any gift of the prince and his followers, but we even rob the Church of its lands and possessions, and strive to abridge or annul its ancient rights and privileges....

The many outrages and disorders which have been the fruits of the new Government of Ireland, are not to be imputed so much to the tender years of the King's son, as to evil counsels, although both had a large share in them; for the land, as yet rude and barbarous, required men of experience, whose minds were matured, to reduce it to order.... But that these great disorders were more to be attributed to the advice of evil counsellors, was even whispered among the younger sort, and taken for certain by older and more discreet persons.

CAPTURE OF JERUSALEM (1187).

Geoffrey de Vinsauf

Source.—*Geoffrey de Vinsauf, Chronicles of the Crusades*, pp. 78-9. G. Bell & Sons.

The fall of Jerusalem was now impending: the victor advancing with speed equal to his hatred, laid siege to the city, and erecting his machines, with sacrilegious irreverence profaned all the holy places. There was a certain cross of stone, which our soldiers formerly, when, after the capture of Antioch, they had gloriously taken this city, had erected on the wall in commemoration of the deed. The ferocious invaders destroyed this cross with a blow from one of their machines, and at the same time struck down a great part of the wall. The citizens interposed such defences as they were able, but all the exertions of our men were ineffectual: bows, balistas and slings were used to no purpose; both arms and machines visibly declared that the Lord was wroth, and foretold the fall of the city. A large number of people had flocked together to the city from the neighbouring fortresses, trusting rather in the sanctity of the place than in the strength of its defences; but in so great a multitude hardly fourteen knights could be found. The priests and clerks, although it was contrary to their profession, discharged the duties of soldiers, according to the emergency, and fought bravely for the Lord's house, bearing in mind the maxim, that to repel force by force is allowed by all laws both human and divine. But the populace alike ignorant and timorous, flocked in numbers round the patriarch and the queen, who were left in charge of the city, bitterly complaining and earnestly entreating that they might treat with the Sultan for peace, as soon as possible. Their capitulation, however, was one to be deplored, rather than praised: for each of them had to pay the ransom of his own life; a man was valued at ten bezants, a woman at five, a child at one; and whoever was unable to pay, was made a slave. It thus happened that when many of them, either out of their own property, or by aids gathered from other sources, had paid the price of their safety, there remained 14,000, who could not redeem themselves and were made slaves for life. To those who purchased their liberty, the choice was given, either to proceed to Antioch, or to be carried under safe-conduct to Alexandria, and thence to cross the sea. That day was indeed a bitter day, on which the exiles separated, each on his different road, and left that sacred city, that city which had been the queen of cities, but which was now reduced to slavery; that city which was the inheritance of its children, but was now in the hands of strangers, on account of the wickedness of those who dwelt therein.

Glorious was Jerusalem, the city of God, where the Lord suffered, and was buried, and where He displayed the glory of His resurrection; but she is now subject to contamination at the hands of her base-born foe; nor is there any grief like that grief, that they should possess the sepulchre, who persecuted Him that lies buried in it; and those, who had despised the Crucified, have made themselves masters of his Cross! This most holy city had been, for about ninety-six years, in the hands of our people, ever since the victorious arms of the Christians had taken it, at the same time as Antioch; when it had been forty years before in the possession of the unbelievers. When the city was taken, the crier of the Mahometan law proceeded to the summit of the rock of Calvary, and there published their false law, in the place where Christ had consummated the law of death upon the cross. Another diabolical act was perpetuated by the enemy. They fastened ropes round a certain cross, which stood upon the pinnacle of the church of the Hospitallers, and dragged it to the ground, where they spat upon it, and hacked it, and drew it, in derision of our faith, through all the filth of the city.

RAISING MONEY FOR THE CRUSADE (1189).

Richard of Devizes

Source.—*Richard of Devizes, Chronicles of the Crusades*, §§ 3, 9, 11, 12. G. Bell & Sons.

3. Now in the year of our Lord's incarnation 1189, Richard, the son of King Henry II. by Eleanor, brother of Henry III.[8] was consecrated King of the English by Baldwin, archbishop of Canterbury, at Westminster, on the 3rd of the Nones of September (3 Sept.). On the very day of the coronation, about that solemn hour, in which the Son was immolated to the Father, a sacrifice of the Jews to their father the devil was commenced in the city of London, and so long was the duration of this famous mystery, that the holocaust could scarcely be accomplished the ensuing day. The other cities and towns of the kingdom emulated the faith of the Londoners, and with a like devotion despatched their bloodsuckers with blood to hell. In this commotion there was prepared, though unequally, some evil against the wicked, everywhere throughout the realm, only Winchester alone, the people being prudent and circumspect, and the city always acting mildly, spared its vermin. It never did anything over speedily; fearing nothing more than to repent, it considers everything before the commencement.

9. The time of commencing his journey pressed hard upon King Richard, as he, who had been first of all the princes on this side the Alps in the taking up of the cross, was unwilling to be last in setting out. A King worthy of the name of King, who, in the first year of his reign, left the kingdom of England for Christ, scarcely otherwise than if he had departed never to return. So great was the devotion of the men, so hastily, so quickly and so speedily did he run, yea fly, to avenge the wrongs of Christ. However, whilst he kept the greater matter in his mind, giving himself in some little measure to deliberation for the kingdom, having received power from the pope that he might withdraw the cross from such of his own subjects as he should desire, for the government of his kingdom, he first appointed Hugh Pudsey, bishop of Durham, to be chief justice of the whole realm, and with design, as is thought by many, further creating him a young earl of Northumberland out of an old bishop, the custody of as many castles as he liked being yielded to him, he diligently cleared from his coffers ten thousand pounds of silver. Geoffrey Fitz-Peter, William Briwere and Hugh Bardulf being permitted to remain at home, the cross being withdrawn from them, the King's treasurer transferred the whole collections of the three as three nuts into the Exchequer. All the sheriffs of

---

[8] Henry, son of King Henry II., is frequently styled Henry the Third, in the early chronicles.

the kingdom on any trivial accusation falling under the King's displeasure, were deprived of their unlucky power, and scarcely permitted to see his face, even by the mediation of inestimable treasure.

11. Godfrey, bishop of Winchester, mindful of his profession, suing for the restoration of the possessions of his church which had been taken away, as no one had any right of replevin against the church of Winchester with respect to its two manors, namely Meones and Weregrave, recovered them by judicial decree, three thousand pounds of silver being privately given to the King. Nor did the considerate man omit at the same time to pay a fine to the King for the indemnity of the church's treasure, for his patrimony, for the county of Hampshire and for the custody of the Castles of Winchester and Porchester. And because the time for the payment of so much money was nigh at hand, as he could not pass over the day fixed for the payment without detriment to the whole business, and he could find no nearer resource under heaven, although against his will, he laid his hand on the treasure of his church, to restore which, however, he obliged himself and his successors, providing security to the convent by the testimony of a sealed bond. A man of such courtesy and moderation, who not even when angry ever did anything to those who were under him, but what savoured of mildness: truly of his family, and one of his familiars, of whom it is said, under whom to live is to reign.

12. The King readily disburthened all whose money was a burthen to them, such powers and possessions as they chose being given to anybody at pleasure; wherewith also on a time an old acquaintance in the company joking him, he broke off with this evasion, "I would sell London if I could find a chapman." Many a one might have been forewarned by that expression, had it been uttered sooner, not to learn to be a wise merchant, after the English proverb, "by buying for a dozen, and selling for one and a half."

LAWS OF RICHARD I. CONCERNING CRUSADERS WHO WERE TO GO BY SEA (1189).

Historical Documents of the Middle Ages

Source.—*Historical Documents of the Middle Ages*, p. 135. Henderson. G. Bell & Sons.

Richard by the grace of God, King of England, and Duke of Normandy and Aquitaine, and Count of Anjou, to all his subjects who are about to go by sea to Jerusalem, greeting. Know that we, by the common counsel of upright men, have made the laws here given. Whoever slays a man on shipboard, shall be bound to the dead man and thrown into the sea. But if he shall slay him on land, he shall be bound to the dead man and buried in the earth. If any one, moreover, shall be convicted through lawful witnesses of having drawn a knife to strike another, or of having struck him so as to draw blood, he shall lose his hand. But if he shall strike him with his fist without drawing blood, he shall be dipped three times in the sea. But if any one shall taunt or insult a comrade or charge him with hatred of God: as many times as he shall have insulted him, so many ounces of silver shall he pay. A robber, moreover, convicted of theft, shall be shorn like a hired fighter, and boiling tar shall be poured over his head, and feathers from a cushion shall be shaken out over his head—so that he may be publicly known; and at the first land where the ships shall put in he shall be cast on shore. Under my own witness at Chinon.

THE ABBOT AND THE JEWS (1190).

Jocelin de Brakelond

Source.—*Jocelin de Brakelond*, Chapter 6. King's Classics. Chatto & Windus.

The lord Abbot sought from the King letters enjoining that the Jews should be driven away from the town of St. Edmund, he stating that whatever is within the town of St. Edmund, or within the banlieue thereof, of right belongs to St. Edmund: therefore the Jews ought to become the men of St. Edmund, otherwise they should be expelled from the town. Licence was accordingly given that he might put them forth, saving, nevertheless, that they had all their chattels and the value of their houses and lands. And when they were expelled, and with an armed force conducted to divers towns, the abbot gave order that all those that from henceforth should harbour or entertain Jews in the town of St. Edmund should be solemnly excommunicated in every church and at every altar. Howbeit it was afterwards conceded by the King's justices that if the Jews should come to the great pleas of the Abbot, to demand their debts from their debtors, on such occasion they might for two days and two nights lodge within the town, and on the third day be permitted to depart freely.'

THE KINGS OF FRANCE AND ENGLAND AT MESSINA (1190).

Geoffrey de Vinsauf

Source. — *Chronicles of the Crusades*, Chap. XIII., pp. 163-4. Bohn's Libraries. G. Bell & Sons.

It is a general custom, that when any particular king or prince of the earth, conspicuous for his glory, might, and authority, comes forth in public, his appearance of power shall not fall short of that with which he is actually invested, — nay, it is but right and becoming that the greatness of a king should be shown in his display and the homage which is paid him; for a common proverb says, "Such as I see you are, I esteem you." Moreover the general style and manner is taken from the disposition of the chief. When, therefore, the King of France, of so high renown, whose edict so many princes and nations obeyed, was known to be entering the port of Messina, the natives, of every age and sex, rushed forth to see so famous a King; but he, content with a single ship, as if to avoid the sight of men, entered the port of the Citadel privately, while those who awaited him along the shore conceived this to be a proof of his weakness, and spoke upbraidingly of him as one not likely to be the performer of any great actions, who thus slunk from the eye of man, and being frustrated in their hopes of seeing him, they returned indignant to their homes. But when the report was spread of the arrival of the noble-minded King of England, the people rushed out eagerly to behold him, crowding along the shore and seating themselves wherever they were likely to catch a glimpse of him. And lo! they beheld the sea in the distance covered with innumerable galleys; and the sound of trumpets and clarions, loud and shrill, strike upon the ear! Then, as they approached nearer, they saw the galleys as they were impelled onward, laden and adorned with arms of all kinds; their pennons and standards floating in countless numbers in the breeze in good order, and on the tops of their spears; the prow of the galleys distinguished from each other by the variety of the paintings, with shields glittering in the sun, and you might behold the sea boiling, from the number of oarsmen who plied it, and the ears of the spectators rang with the peals of the instruments commonly called trumpets, and their delight was aroused by the approach of the varied crowd, when lo! the magnificent King, accompanied by the crowd of obedient galleys, standing on a prow more elevated and ornamental than the others, as if to see what he had not seen before, or to be seen by the crowds that densely thronged the shore, lands in a splendid dress, where the sailors whom he had sent before him, and others of his equipage, receive him with congratulations, and bring forward the chargers and horses which had been committed to their care for transportation, that he and his suite might mount. The natives crowd round him on all sides, mixed with his own men, and followed him to his hostel. The common people conversed with each other in admiration of his great glory; and agreed that he was worthy of Empire, and deserved to be set over nations and kingdoms, "for the fame of him which we had before heard fell far short of the truth when we saw him." Meanwhile, the trumpets blew, and their sounds being harmoniously blended, there arose a kind of discordant concord of notes. Whilst the sameness of the sounds being continued, the one followed the other in mutual succession, and the notes which had been lowered were again resounded.

THE CAPTURE OF MESSINA,
AND THE JEALOUSY OF PHILIP,
KING OF FRANCE (1190).

Geoffrey de Vinsauf

Source.—*Chronicles of the Crusades*, pp. 169-70. Bohn's Libraries. G. Bell & Sons.

King Richard captured Messina by one assault, in less time than a priest could chant the matin service. Many more of the citizens would have fallen, had not King Richard, with an impulse of generosity, ordered their lives to be spared. But who could reckon the sum of money which the citizens lost? All the gold and silver, and whatsoever precious thing was found became the property of the victors. They also set fire to, and burnt to ashes, the enemy's galleys, lest they should escape, and recover strength to resist. The victors also carried off their noblest women. And lo! after this action had been performed, the French suddenly beheld the ensigns and standards of King Richard floating above the walls of the city; at which the King of France was so mortified, that he conceived that hatred against King Richard which lasted during his life, and afterwards led him to the unjust invasion of Normandy.

Chap. XVII. The King of France, jealous of the successes of the King of England, and misliking his high spirit, very much grieved that he should not have the glory which the other had gained by the force of his own greatness; for, contrary to the conditions of mutual agreement, and while the army was in the greatest danger, and a great slaughter going on before his eyes, he proffered not a helping hand to the King of England against an obstinate foe. As he was bound by the treaty of alliance. Nay, he resisted as much as he could, and kept him a long time from occupying the entrance of the city where he himself abode. The city being taken, as we said before, and the banners of King Richard planted on the walls, the King of France, as an acknowledgment of his superiority, ordered his banners to be planted above those of the English King. King Richard, indignant at this command, considering what previously occurred, and bearing in mind the rights of their fellowship, sent no answer, lest he should seem to surrender his right, and the victory should be ascribed not only to one who had been inactive, but to a perjured adversary. At the intercession of mediators, however, the anger of King Richard, was at length appeased; an end was put to their wrangling, and, yielding to the soothings of his friends, with some difficulty, he was held invincible, being overcome by his foes, gave way to the request of the King of France, viz. that he should deliver into his custody the towers he had taken, and place in them guards of both nations, until they should learn the sentiments of King Tancred as to what had been done; and he who remained angry and obdurate to threats and boastings was moved by prayers and soothing. The standards of both were, therefore, raised above the walls of the city, until he should try the constancy of the King of France, and prove his friendship.

CAPTURE OF CYPRUS AND RICHARD'S MARRIAGE, 1191.

Richard of Devizes

Source.—*Richard of Devizes*, §§ 59, 61, *Chronicles of the Crusades*. Bohn's Libraries. G. Bell & Sons.

59. The fleet of Richard, King of the English, put out to sea, and proceeded in this order. In the fore-front went three ships only, in one of which was the Queen of Sicily and the young damsel of Navarre, probably still a virgin; in the other two a certain part of the King's treasure and arms; in each of the three, marines and provisions. In the second line there were, what with ships and busses and men of war, thirteen; in the third, fourteen; in the fourth, twenty; in the fifth, thirty; in the sixth, forty; in the seventh, sixty; in the last, the King himself, followed with his galleys.

60. Now as the ships were proceeding in the aforesaid manner and order, some being before others, two of the three first, driven by the violence of the winds, were broken on the rocks near the port of Cyprus; the third, which was English, more speedy than they, having turned back into the deep, escaped the peril. Almost all the men of both ships got away alive to land, many of whom the hostile Cypriotes slew, some they took captive, some, taking refuge in a certain church, were besieged. Whatever also in the ships was cast up by the sea, fell a prey to the Cypriotes.... God so willed that the cursed people should receive the reward of their evil deeds by the hands of one who would not spare. The third English ship, in which were the women, having cast out its anchors, rode out at sea, and watched all things from opposite, to report the misfortune to the King, lest haply, being ignorant of the loss and disgrace, he should pass the place unrevenged. The next line of the King's ships came up after the other, and they all stopped at the first. A full report reached the King, who, sending heralds to the lord of the island, and obtaining no satisfaction, commanded his entire army to arm, from the first even to the last, and to get out of the great ships into the galleys and boats, and follow him to the shore. What he commanded, was immediately performed; they came in arms to the port. The King being armed, leaped first from his galley, and gave the first blow in the war; but before he was able to strike a second, he had three thousand of his followers with him, striking away by his side. All the timber that had been placed as a barricade in the port was cast down instantly, and the brave fellows went up into the city, as ferocious as lionesses are wont to be when robbed of their young. The fight was carried on manfully against them, numbers fell down

wounded on both sides, and the swords of both parties were made drunk with blood. The Cypriotes are vanquished, the city is taken, with the castle besides; whatever the victors choose is ransacked, and the lord of the island is himself taken and brought to the King. He, being taken, supplicates and obtains pardon; he offers homage to the King, and it is received; and he swears, though unasked, that henceforth he will hold the island of him as his liege lord, and will open all the castles of the land to him, make satisfaction for the damage already done; and further, bring presents of his own. On being dismissed after the oath, he is commanded to fulfil the conditions in the morning.

61. That night the King remained peaceably in the castle; and his newly-sworn vassal flying, retired to another castle, and caused the whole of the men of that land, who were able to bear arms, to be summoned to repair to him, and so they did. The King of Jerusalem, however, that same night, landed in Cyprus, that he might assist the King and salute him, whose arrival he had desired above that of any other in the whole world. On the morrow, the lord of Cyprus was sought for and found to have fled. The King, seeing that he was abused and having been informed where he was, directed the King of Jerusalem to follow the traitor by land with the half of the army, while he conducted the other part by water, intending to be in the way, that he might not escape by sea. The divisions reassembled around the city in which he had taken refuge, and he, having sallied out against the King, fought with the English, and the battle was carried on sharply by both sides. The English would that day have been beaten, had they not fought under the command of King Richard. They at length obtained a dear-bought victory, the Cypriote flies, and the castle is taken. The Kings pursue him as before, the one by land, the other by water, and he is besieged in the third castle. Its walls are cast down by engines hurling huge stones; he, being overcome, promises to surrender, if only he might not be put in iron fetters. The King consents to the prayers of the supplicant, and caused silver shackles to be made for him. The prince of the pirates being thus taken, the King traversed the whole island, and took all its castles, and placed his constables in each, and constituted justiciaries and sheriffs; and the whole land was subjected to him in everything just like England. The gold, and the silk, and the jewels from the treasures that were broken open, he retained for himself; the silver and victuals he gave to the army. To the King of Jerusalem also he made a handsome present out of his booty.

And because Lent had already passed, and the lawful time of contract was come, he caused Berengaria, daughter of the King of Navarre, whom his mother had brought to him in Lent, to be affianced to him in the island.

AT ACRE (1191).

Geoffrey de Vinsauf

Source.—*Geoffrey de Vinsauf*, Chs. IV., V., VI., VIII., *Chronicles of the Crusades.* Bohn's Libraries. G. Bell & Sons.

On the following day of Pentecost, King Richard arrived with an army, the flower of war, and upon learning that the King of France had gained the goodwill and favour of all, by giving to each of his soldiers three "aurei" a month,—not to be outdone or equalled in generosity, he proclaimed by mouth of herald, that whosoever was in his service, no matter of what nation, should receive four statute "aurei" a month for his pay. By these means his generosity was extolled by all, for he outshone everyone else in merit and favours, as he outdid them in gifts and magnificence. "When," exclaimed they, "will the first attack take place, by a man whom we have expected so long and anxiously? A man, by far the first of kings, and the most skilled in war throughout Christendom? Now let the will of God be done, for the hope of all rests on King Richard." But after some days sojourn, the King was afflicted with a severe illness, to which the common people gave the name of Arnoldia, which is produced by change of climate working on the con-stitution. But for all that, he caused petrariae and mangonels to be raised, and a fort in front of the city gates; and spared no pains to expedite the construction of machines.

Ch. V. The King of France, not liking the delay in commencing the attack, sent word to King Richard, that a favourable opportunity now offered itself: and he also warned, by voice of herald, the army to prepare for an assault. But King Richard had signified his inability hitherto to attend to his duty, both on account of indisposition, and because his men were not yet come; though he hoped that they would arrive in the next fleet of ships, and would bring with them materials for the construction of machines. The King of France, not thinking fit to desist, on that account, from his purpose, commanded an assault to be proclaimed, by voice of herald throughout the army. Therefore, on the Monday after the Feast of the Nativity of St. John the Baptist, the King of France, having erected his machines, gave orders to his men to arm. Then might have been seen a countless multitude of armed men, worthily equipped; and so many coats of scale armour, gleaming hel-mets, and noble chargers with pennons and banners of various workmanship, and soldiers of tried valour and courage, as never had been seen before. Having placed men to defend the trenches against the threatened attack of Saladin from without, the armies approached the walls of the city and commenced a most vigorous as-sault, by casting darts and stones from arbalests and machines, without ceasing.

When the Turks who were shut up in the city saw this, they raised a tumultuous clamour and shouted to the skies; so that it resembled the crash in the air caused by thunder and lightning; for some had this sole duty—to beat basins and platters; to strike timbrels; and by other means to make signal to Saladin and the army without; in order that they might come to their succour, according to agreement. And when the Turks from without saw and heard this, they gathered in a body; and collecting every material within their reach to fill up the ditch, they essayed to cross over, and attack our men, but failed in effecting their object. For Godfrey of Lusignan, a man of the most approved valour, opposed them, and drove them back from the barricades, which they had already seized upon, above our men; and he slew ten of them with an axe he carried in his hand, in a most glorious manner; and none he smote escaped; nay, he took some alive; for such was his courage and activity, that no one since the time of those famous soldiers, Roland and Oliver, could lay claim to such distinction, from the mouth of all, as himself. Our men regained the barricades, but with much labour and difficulty; for the Turks kept pouring in, and by their obstinate persistence, made the issue a long time doubtful. So severe and insupportable was the struggle, and so horrible the clamour of the conflict, that the men who were making the assault on the city and were intent on filling up the trenches, were forced to retire and give up the attempt, for they were not able to carry on the assault, and at the same time defend their camp from the Turks without. And many of the French perished from the darts cast by the arbalests, the throwing of stones, and the pouring on them of Greek fire; and there was great mourning and lamentation among the people. O! with what earnestness had we expected the arrival of the Kings! How fallen were our hopes! They had come, and we profited not; nay, we suffered a severer loss than usual; and those we expected came to no purpose. Our men of France having laid aside their arms, the Turks began to revile them shamefully; and reproached them with not being able to accomplish what they had begun; moreover, they threw Greek fire on the machines and other warlike instruments of the King of France, which had been made with such care, and destroyed them. Whence the King of France, overcome by fury and anger, sunk into a state of languid sickness, from sorrow, it was said; and from confusion and discouragement, mounted not on horseback.

Ch. VIII. The City of Acre, from its strong position, and its being defended by the choicest men of the Turks, appeared difficult to be taken by assault. The French had hitherto spent their labour in vain in constructing machines and engines for breaking down the walls, with the greatest care; for whatever they erected, at a great expense, the Turks destroyed with Greek fire or some devouring conflagration. Amongst other machines and engines which the King of France had erected for breaking down the walls, he had prepared one with great labour, to be used for scaling it, which they called a "cat," because like a cat it crept up and adhered to the wall. He had also another, made of strong hurdle twigs, put together most compactly, which they used to call a "cercleia," and under its covering of hides the King of France used to sit, and employ himself in throwing darts from a sling; he would thus watch the approach of the Turks, above on the walls, by the battlements, and then hit them unawares. But it happened one day that the French were eagerly pressing forward to apply their cat to the walls, when behold! the Turks let down upon it a heap of the driest wood, and threw upon it a quantity of Greek fire, as well as upon the hurdle they had constructed with such toil, and then aimed a petraria in that direction, and all having forthwith caught fire, they broke them in pieces by the blows from their petraria. Upon this the King of France was enraged beyond measure, and began to curse all those who were under his command; and rated them shamefully for not exacting condign vengeance of the Saracens, who had done them such injuries. In the heat of his passion, and when the day was drawing in, he published an edict, by voice of herald, that an assault should be made upon the city on the morrow.

Ch. XV. What can we say of this race of unbelievers who thus defended their city? They must be admired for their valour in war, and were the honour of their whole nation. Yet they dreaded our men, not without reason, for they saw the choicest soldiers from the ranks of all Christendom come to destroy them; their walls in part broken down, in part shattered, the greater portion of their army mutilated, some killed, and others weakened by their wounds. There were still remaining in the city 6000 Turks, with Mestoc and Caracois their chiefs, but they despaired of succour. They perceived that the Christian army was very much dejected at the death of Alberic Clements, and their sons and kinsmen who had fallen in battle, and that they were determined either to die bravely, or gain the mastery over the Turks, and that they thought a middle course dishonourable. Under these circumstances, by common counsel and assent, the besieged begged a truce, in order to inform Saladin of their condition, and to ascertain how far he would afford them security according to the manner of barbarous nations, by either sending them speedy help, or giving them leave to depart from the city with honour. To obtain this object, two of the most noble of the Saracens and of Paganism, Mestoc and Caracois, came to our Kings with the promise that if Saladin did not send them speedy assistance, they would give up the city, on the condition that all the besieged Turks should be permitted to depart in freedom, with their arms and property, and go whithersoever they liked. And on the King of France and nearly all the French giving their assent to this condition at the conference, King Richard absolutely refused his, and said, it was not to be consented to, that after so long and laborious a siege they should enter a deserted city only. On his pleasure being known, Caracois and Mestoc returned to the city without effecting their object. And Saladin, when he learnt that ambassadors had been sent by the besieged, commanded them to persevere and defend their city with as much courage as that which they had hitherto shewn, promising that most ample assistance should soon come to them without a doubt; for he declared to the ambassadors who waited upon him that he would certainly persevere, and as he was expecting a large body of soldiers from Babylon, they would soon come in ships and galleys; for he had given orders to Muleina to be with him, without fail, in eight days; and if they did not come according to agreement, he promised with an oath to procure for them as honourable a peace as he could from the Christians, and the liberty to depart. On hearing these things, the ambassadors returned to the city, and, repeating the promises of Saladin, persuaded the townsmen to resist while they looked forward with anxiety for the promised assistance.

Ch. XVI. Meanwhile, the petrariae of the Christians never ceased, day and night, to shake the walls; and when the Turks saw this, they were smitten with wonder, astonishment, terror, and confusion; and many, yielding to their fears, threw themselves down from the walls by night, and without waiting for the promised aid, very many sought, with supplications, the sacrament of baptism and Christianity....

Ch. XVII. Saladin, perceiving the dangers of delay, at length determined to yield to the entreaties of the besieged; he was, moreover, persuaded by his admirals, and his satraps, and his influential courtiers, who had many friends and kinsmen among the besieged. The latter alleged also, that he was bound to them on his promise made on the Mahometan law, that he would procure for them an honourable capitulation at the last moment, lest, perchance, made prisoners at discretion, they should be exterminated or put to an ignominious death, and thus the law of Mahomet, which had been strictly observed by their ancestors, be effaced by its dependence on him; and nevertheless very much would be derogated from his name and excellence if the worshippers of Mahomet should fall into the hands of Christians. They also begged to remind Saladin of the fact that they, a chosen race of Turks, in obedience to his commands, had been cooped up in the city, and withstood a siege for so long a time; they reminded him too, that they had not seen their wives and children for three years, during which period the siege had lasted; and they said that it would be better to surrender the city, than that people of such merit should be destroyed. The princes persuading the Sultan to this effect, that their latter condition might not be worse than their former one; he assented to their making peace on the best terms they could, and they drew up a statement of what appeared to them the most proper terms of treaty....

Ch. XVIII. Thus, after the Friday after the Translation of St. Benedict, the principal and noblest of the admirals were given and received as hostages, and the space of one month fixed for the delivery of the Cross and the collecting together of the captives. And when it was rumoured abroad that the city was to be given up, the common people, in their folly, were inflamed with fury, but the wiser portion rejoiced, at gaining so profitably and without danger, what they had been so long a time unable to obtain. Then was it proclaimed and prohibited by voice of herald, that any one should molest the Turks by word or deed, or provoke them by abuse, or that missiles should any longer be cast for the destruction of the walls or of the Turks who might be seen on the battlements.

RETURN OF PHILIP (1191).

Geoffrey de Vinsauf

Source.—*Geoffrey de Vinsauf*, Ch. XXI., *Chronicles of the Crusades*. Bohn's Libraries. G. Bell & Sons.

Ch. XXI. Affairs being in this position, at the end of the month of July, within which the Turks had promised to restore the holy cross, and receive back their hostages, a rumour spread among the army, that the King of France, on whom the hope of the people rested, intended to return home, and was making active preparations for his journey. Oh how wicked and how insulting a proceeding, while as yet so much work remained on hand, to wish to go away, when his duty was to rule so large a multitude of people, and when his presence was so necessary to encourage the Christians to so pious a work, and to provide for the progress of so arduous an undertaking! O why did he come so long a way and with so much toil, if he intended to return almost immediately? O wonderful performance of his vow, by merely entering the Holy Land, and contending against the Turks with such small triumph! But why need we say more? The King of France alleged sickness as the cause of his return; and said that he had performed his vow as far as he was able; most of all, because he was well and sound when he took up the cross with King Henry between Trie and Gisors.... But when the inflexible determination of the King of France to return became known to all, and his refusal to yield to the murmurs of his men, or their supplications to remain, the French would have renounced their subjection to him, if it could have been done, and would have loathed his dominion; and they imprecated on him every kind of adversity and misfortune that could fall to the lot of man in this life. But for all that the King of France hastened his voyage as much as possible, and left in his stead the Duke of Burgundy, with a large number of men. Moreover, he begged King Richard to supply him with two galleys, and the King readily gave him two of his best; how ungrateful he was of this service was afterwards seen.

RICHARD'S SICKNESS (1192). A TRUCE.

Richard of Devizes

Source.—*Richard of Devizes*, §§ 87, 88, 90, 91, 92, 93, *Chronicles of the Crusades.*
Bohn's Libraries. G. Bell & Sons.

§ 87. The King was extremely sick, and confined to his bed; his fever continued without intermission; the physicians whispered that it was an acute semitertian.... No one speaks of the indisposition of the King, lest the secret of their intense sorrow should be disclosed to the enemy; for it was thoroughly understood that Saladin feared the charge of the whole army less than that of the King alone; and if he should know that he was dead, he would instantly pelt the French with cow-dung, and intoxicate the best of the English with a dose that should make them tremble.

§ 88. In the meantime, a certain Gentile, called Saffatin, came down to see the King as he generally did: he was a brother of Saladin, an ancient man of war of remarkable politeness and intelligence, and one whom the King's magnanimity and munificence had charmed even to the love of his person and favour of his party. The King's servants greeting him less joyfully than they were accustomed, and not admitting him to an interview with the King, "I perceive," said he by his interpreter, "that you are greatly afflicted; nor am I ignorant of the cause. My friend your King is sick.... O! if that Richard, whom although I love yet I fear, if he were despatched out of the way, how little should we then fear, how very little should we make account of that youngest of the sons, who sleeps at home in clover. It was not unknown to us, that Richard, who nobly succeeded his great father in the kingdom, immediately set forward against us even in the very year of his coronation. The number of his ships and troops was not unknown to us before his setting forth. We knew, even at the very time, with what speed he took Messina. The well-fortified city of Sicily, which he besieged; and although none of our people believed it, yet our fears increased, and fame added false terrors to the true.

§ 91. "His valour unable to rest in one place, proceeded through a boundless region, and everywhere left trophies of his courage. We questioned among ourselves whether he made ready to subdue, for his God the Land of Promise only, or at the same time to take the whole world for himself. Who shall worthily relate the capture of Cyprus? Verily had the island of Cyprus been close to Egypt, and had my brother Saladin subdued it in ten years, his name would have been reckoned by the people among the names of the gods. When, however, we at last perceived that he overthrew whatever resisted his purpose, our hearts were melted as the hoar-frost melts at the appearance of the approaching sun, forasmuch as it was said of him that he ate his enemies alive. And if he were not presently, on the very day of his arrival before Acre, received freely into the city with open gates, fear alone was the cause. It was not from their desire to preserve the city, but through dread of the torments promised them and their despair of life that they fought so bravely, or rather, desperately, fearing this more than death, endeavouring this by all means, namely, that they should not die unrevenged. And this was not from sheer obstinacy, but to follow up the doctrine of our faith. For we believe that the spirits of the unavenged wander for ever, and that they are deprived of all rest. But what did the rashness and timidity of the devoted profit them? Being vanquished by force and constrained by fear to surrender, they were punished with a more lenient death than they expected. And yet, oh! shame on the Gentiles, their spirits wandered unavenged! I swear to you by the Great God, that if, after he had gained Acre, he had immediately led his army to Jerusalem, he would not have found even one of our people in the whole circuit of the Christian's land; on the contrary, we should have offered him inestimable treasure, that he might not proceed, that he might not prosecute us further.

§ 92. "But thanks be to God, he was burdened with the King of the French, and hindered by him like a cat with a hammer tied to its tail. To conclude, we, though his rivals, see nothing in Richard that we can find fault with but his valour; nothing to hate but his experience in war. But what glory is there in fighting with a sick man? And although this very morning I could have wished that both you and he had all received your final doom, now I compassionate you on account of your King's illness. I will either obtain for you a settled peace with my brother, or at the least, a good and durable truce...."

§ 93. The bishop of Salisbury and such of the most trusty of the King's household as were present, who had secretly deliberated with him upon this subject, reluctantly consented to the truce which before they had determined to purchase at any price, as if it had been detested and not desired by them. So their right hands being given and received, Saffatin, when he had washed his face, and disguised his sorrow, returned to Jerusalem, to Saladin. The council was assembled before his brother, and after seventeen days of weighty argument, he with difficulty succeeded in prevailing on the stubbornness of the Gentiles to grant a truce to the Christians. The time was appointed and the form approved. If it please King Richard, for the space of three years, three months, three weeks, three days and three hours, such a truce shall be observed between the Christians and the Gentiles, that whatever either one party or the other in any wise possesses, he shall possess without molestation to the end; it will be permitted during the interval, that the Christians at their pleasure may fortify Acre only, and the Gentiles Jerusalem. All contracts, commerce, every act and every thing shall be mutually carried on by all in peace. Saffatin himself is despatched to the English as the bearer of this decree.

CHIVALRY OF SALADIN (1192-3).

Geoffrey de Vinsauf

Source.—*Geoffrey de Vinsauf*, Ch. 32, *Chronicles of the Crusades*. Bohn's Libraries. G. Bell & Sons.

The next day certain of the Turks appeared before Saladin, and earnestly entreated of him that they might be allowed to take vengeance on the Christians who were now in their power, for the death of their friends, fathers, brothers, sons, and relations who had been slain, first at Acre, and afterwards at other places, and now, as they said, that they had so good an opportunity. Saladin sent for the Turkish chiefs to consult about this request, and Mestoc, Saphadin, Bedridin, and Dorderin, were speedily in attendance. When the subject was placed before them, it was their unanimous opinion that the Christians should have leave to come and go, without injury or hinderance. "For," said they to Saladin, "it would be a deep stain upon our honour, if the treaty which has been made between you and the King of England should, by our interference, be broken, and the faith of the Turks for ever afterwards be called in question." In consequence of these observations, Saladin gave orders immediately that the Christians should be taken care of, and escorted to the city and back again without molestation. To discharge this commission, Saphadin was at his own request deputed; and under his protection the pilgrims had free access to the Holy Sepulchre, and were treated with the greatest liberality, after which they returned joyfully to Acre.

RETURN OF RICHARD (1193).

Geoffrey de Vinsauf

Source.—*Geoffrey de Vinsauf*, Ch. 37, *Chronicles of the Crusades*. Bohn's Libraries. G. Bell & Sons.

Everything was now settled, and the King was already on the point of embarking, when determining before he went, to leave nothing behind him which might detract from his honour, he ordered proclamation to be made that all who had claims on him should come forward, and that all his debts should be paid fully, and more than fully, to avoid all occasion afterwards of detraction or complaint. What sighs and tears were there when the royal fleet weighed anchor! A blessing was invoked on the King's many acts of benevolence, his virtues and his largesses were set forth, and the numerous excellences combined in one man. How then did the lamentations of all resound as they exclaimed, O Jerusalem, bereft now of every succour! How hast thou lost thy defender? Who will protect thee, should the truce be broken, now that King Richard is departed? Such were the words of each when the King, whose health was not yet fully re-established, and who was the subject of all their anxious wishes, went on board and set sail. All night the ship ran on her way by the light of the stars, and when morning dawned, the King looked back with yearning eyes upon the land which he had left, and after long meditation, he prayed aloud, in the hearing of several, in these words: "O holy land, I commend thee to God, and if his heavenly grace shall grant me so long to live, that I may in his good pleasure, afford thee assistance, I hope, as I propose to be able to be some day a succour to thee." With these words he urged the sailors to spread their canvass to the winds, that they might the sooner cross over the expanse of sea that lay before them; ignorant indeed of the tribulations and sorrows which awaited him, and the calamities that he was to suffer from the treachery that had long before been transmitted to France, by which it was contrived that he should be wickedly thrown into prison, though he justly suspected no such evil in the service of God, and in so laborious a pilgrimage. O how unequally was he recompensed for his exertions in the common cause! His inheritance was seized by another, his castles in Normandy were unjustly taken, his rivals made cruel assaults on his rights without provocation, and he only escaped from captivity by paying a ransom to the Emperor of Germany. To gather the money for his ransom, the taxes were raised to the uttermost; a large collection was levied upon all his land and everything was distracted; for the chalices and hallowed vessels of gold and silver were gathered from the churches, and the monasteries were obliged to do without their utensils; neither was this unlawful according to the decrees of the holy fathers, nay, it was even a matter of necessity inasmuch as no saint, many though there be, ever during life, suffered so much for the Lord as King Richard in his captivity in Austria and in Germany. He who had gained so many triumphs over the Turks was nefariously circumvented by the brethren of his own faith, and seized by those who agreed with him in name only as members of the Creed of Christ. Alas, how much more are secret snares to be feared than open discord, according to the proverb, "It is easier to avoid a hostile than a deceitful man." Oh, shame be it said, that one whom no adversary could resist, nor the whole force of Saladin could conquer, was now seized by an ignoble people, and kept a prisoner in Germany. Oh, how painful is it for those who have been nurtured in liberty, to be placed at the beck of another! But out of that captivity, by God's usual mercy, his own activity, and the care of his faithful servants, he was at length set at liberty for a large sum of money, because he was known to be a man of great power. At last restored to his native soil and the kingdom of his ancestors, in a short time he restored all to tranquillity. He then crossed over into Normandy, to avenge himself on the wanton aggressions of the King of France, his rival; and when he had more than once defeated him, he powerfully recovered with sword and spear his alienated rights, even with augmentation.

RICHARD'S CAPTURE (1192).

Roger de Hoveden

Source.—*Roger de Hoveden*, Vol. II., pp. 269-70. Bohn's Libraries. G. Bell & Sons.

After this, the King of England placing everything in the hands of Henry, Count of Champagne, hastened to return to his kingdom, by reason of the sinister reports which he had heard, both as to the King of France and the expulsion of his Chancellor, as also the Earl of Mortaigne, his brother, who had seized the castles of the kingdom and would have taken possession of the whole thereof if he could have found the opportunity. Accordingly, the King of England came to Caiaphas, where he fell sick, and proceeded thence to Acre. Here, after the feast of St. Michael, being the eighth day before the Ides of October, and the fifth day of the week, he embarked on board of a large buss, and, within a month from that day, arrived at the island of Cunerfu, where he went on board a boat, and sailed towards three galleys which he saw on the opposite side off the coast of Romania, and hired them to take him as far as Ragusa, for two hundred marks of silver; after which he returned to his buss, and the said galleys with him; and, having made terms with them, he took with him Baldwin, the advocate of Bethune, and twenty other companions, and embarked on board one of the said galleys, and on landing at Gazera, near Ragusa, declined to tell them that he was King of England, but said that they were pilgrims. However, although he had a long beard and long hair and garments, and everything else to resemble the people of that country, he was unable to remain unknown, in consequence of his great expenditure, which was quite foreign to the usage of the people of that country.

Immediately, the people of the province guessing that he was the King of England, prepared to capture him and deliver him to the Emperor of the Romans, who hated him, on account of the aid he had given to King Tancred, and for the death of his kinsman, the Marquis Conrad. Upon the King of England being informed of this by one of his followers, he placed his retinue in charge of Baldwin, the Advocate of Bethune, and ordered him to remain the next four days at that place, making a more lavish expenditure than he himself had done; after which, he himself, with a single attendant, having mounted a swift horse, his attendant doing the same, set out late at night, and, hastening day and night, arrived in the neighbourhood of Vienna; at a little village, not far from which place he and his attendant took up their abode. While the King's attendant was gone to buy food, the King, being fatigued by the labour of his journey, immediately threw himself upon a bed and fell asleep. In the meantime, his attendant, while endeavouring to exchange some money, was recognized by the servant of the duke of Austria, and taken prisoner, and brought before the duke; and, when he could conceal it no longer, disclosed to him the lodging of the King; on which they came, and, finding him asleep, took him prisoner. As for the Advocate of Bethune, and those who were with him, on attempting to leave the town, they were taken prisoners, and not allowed to depart.

THE RELEASE OF RICHARD (1192).

Roger de Hoveden

Source.—*Roger de Hoveden*, Vol. II., pp. 281-2. Bohn's Libraries. G. Bell & Sons.

Accordingly, upon hearing of the confinement of the King, Walter, Archbishop of Rouen, and the other justiciaries of our lord the King, sent the Abbot of Boxley and the Abbot of Pont Robert to Germany, to seek the King of England. After having passed through the whole of Germany, and not finding the King, they entered Bavaria, and met the King at a town, the name of which is Oxefer, where he was brought before the Emperor, to hold a conference with him, on Palm Sunday. On hearing that the before-named abbots had come from England, the King showed himself courteous and affable to them; making enquiries about the state of his kingdom and the fidelity of his subjects, and the health and prosperity of the King of Scotland, in whose fidelity he placed a very strong reliance: on which they testified to what they had heard and seen. A conference accordingly taking place between them, the King made complaint of the treachery of his brother, John, earl of Mortaigne, on whom he had conferred so many favours and boundless honors, and who had thrown himself into the hands of the King of France against him, and, having broken the ties of brotherhood, had made a league with death and a compact with hell. The King, though greatly afflicted upon this subject, suddenly broke forth into these words of consolation, saying, "My brother John is not the man to subjugate a country, if there is a person able to make the slightest resistance to his attempts."

During his journey of three days, while on the road to meet the emperor, it was the admiration of all how boldly, how courteously, and how becomingly he behaved himself, and they judged him worthy of the imperial elevation who so thoroughly understood the arts of command, and how, with uniform self-possession, to rise superior to the two-faced events of fortune. On a day named, after he had held a conference by messengers with the emperor, they were unable on that day to have an interview with him, because the Emperor had made of him many demands, to which the King had determined not to yield, even though his life should be perilled thereby. On the morrow, however, while all were despairing, with joyous success ensued joyous consolation.

For, on the emperor accusing the King of many things, and charging him with many misdeeds, both with his betrayal of the land of Sulia, and with the death of the Marquis of Montferrat, as also with reference to certain covenants made between them and not observed by him, the King made answer with such frankness, such self-possession and such intrepidity, that the emperor thought him worthy, not only of his favour and pardon, but even of his praise. For he raised the King when bending before him, and received him with the kiss of peace, and made a treaty of friendship with him, and, loading him with honors and succour (the people standing round and bursting into tears for very joy), made a promise that he would reconcile the King of England with the King of France. After this, with the mediation of the duke of Austria, the King of England promised that he would pay to the Emperor for his liberation, by way of ransom, one hundred thousand marks. The emperor also promised that, if by his means the King of England and the King of France could not be reconciled, he would send the King of England home without exacting the money.

ENGLAND UNDER THE CHANCELLORS (1191-3).

Roger de Hoveden

Source.—*Roger de Hoveden*, Vol. II., p. 231 *seqq*. Bohn's Libraries. G. Bell & Sons.

William, bishop of Ely, the King's Chancellor, was a great man among all the people of the west, and, as though gifted with a two-fold right hand, wielded the power of the kingdom, and the authority of the Apostolic See, and was in possession of the King's seal over all lands, so as to be enabled to govern according to his own will, and of his own power to bring all things to completion; even in the same degree of estimation as both king and priest together was he held; nor was there any person to be found to dare to offer resistance to his will. For he said, and the thing was done, he commanded, and all means were discovered. In his hands were the royal treasures, the whole of the King's riches, and the entire exchequer, so much so that all property whatsoever that swam beneath our skies was no longer said to belong to the King, but to him. And really if it had been the time of the Cæsars, he would with Tiberius have had himself styled the living God. But when the King had given him certain earls as his associates, in order that at least the more weighty concerns of the realm might be managed by their counsels in common, he could not at all endure to have any partner therein, as he thought that the greater part of his glory would be thrown into the shade, if he should stand in need of the advice of any mortal being. Therefore he ruled alone, therefore he reigned alone, and from sea to sea was he dreaded as though a God; and were I to say still more, I should not be telling a falsehood, because God is long-suffering and merciful; while he, ruling every thing according to his own impulses, was neither able to observe justice when acting, nor to endure delay in waiting the proper time. Hence it arose that he set at nought all the letters and mandates of his lord; that he might not seem to have a superior nor be supposed to be subject to any one, having always made every one act as the servant of his own will. Therefore, after England had for a considerable time suffered under so heavy a burden and a yoke so insupportable, at length, while groaning at his deeds, she cried aloud with all her might. As, therefore, a man so powerful could not be overcome by man, the Father of Mercies and the God of all consolation came to the aid of the people who supplicated God, and supplanting the hand of mercy in his case, hurled him down from his power, and brought this accuser, or rather destroyer, to such a pitch of giddiness of mind, that he was unable to recover or rouse himself therefrom; but he so hardened his heart, blinded his mind, and infatuated his counsels, that he first besieged the Archbishop of York in a church, then seized him, and after seizing him, violently tore him away; after tearing him away, strongly bound him; after strongly binding him, dragged him along; and after dragging him along, threw him into prison. And although there was a concourse of people who exclaimed, "What has this righteous man and friend of God been guilty of, that he should be taken to prison? his innocent blood is condemned without a cause." Still pity could not listen where pride reigned, and God was not heard where the tyrant held sway. For the said Archbishop was coming from the country of Normandy with his pastoral staff and mitre, and ring, and superhumeral, which in later times has been styled the pall. And although he was the son of King Henry, of happy memory, and the brother of King Richard, who now reigns, and the brother of John, Earl of Mortaigne, still, his royal blood could be of no service to him; and although he had been recently consecrated, the recent performance of that sacrament could not avail him.

The associates also of the said Chancellor whom the King had associated with him in the government of the kingdom, accused him of many offences, saying that, despising their advice, he had transacted all the affairs of the kingdom according to impulse and his own will. The Archbishop of Rouen also, and William Marshal, Earl of Striguil, then for the first time produced before the people the sealed letters from our lord the King, in which the King had sent orders from Messina, that they should be associated with him in the government of the kingdom, and that, without the advice of them and the other persons so appointed, he was not to act in the affairs of the King and the kingdom, and that if he should do anything to the detriment of the kingdom, or without the consent of the persons before-named, he should be deposed and the Archbishop of Rouen substituted in his place.

It seemed good, therefore, to John, the King's brother, and all the bishops, earls, and barons of the kingdom, and to the citizens of London, that the Chancellor should be deposed, and they accordingly deposed him, and substituted in his place the Archbishop of Rouen, who was willing to do nothing in the government of kingdom except with the will and consent of the persons assigned to him as associates therein, and with the sanction of the barons of the exchequer.

THE CAPTURE OF ARTHUR (1202).

Roger of Wendover

Source.—*Roger of Wendover*, Vol. II., *Annal 1202.* Bohn's Libraries. G. Bell & Sons.

When the French and the people of Poictou learned that the King was on his way, they went out with a pompous array to meet him, and give him battle; but when they met each other in battle order, and had engaged, the King bravely withstood their turbulent attacks, and at length put them to flight, pursuing them so quickly with his cavalry, that he entered the castle at the same time as the fugitives. Then a most severe conflict took place inside the walls of the castle, but was soon determined by the laudable valour of the English: in the conflict there two hundred French knights were taken prisoners, and all the nobles in Poictou and Anjou, together with Arthur himself, so that not one out of the whole number escaped, who could return and tell the misfortune to the rest of their countrymen. Having, therefore, secured his prisoners in fetters and shackles, and placed them in cars, a new and unusual mode of conveyance, the King sent some of them to Normandy, and some to England, to be imprisoned in strong castles, whence there would be no fear of their escape; but Arthur was kept at Falaise under close custody.

THE LOSS OF NORMANDY (1204).

Roger of Wendover

Source.—*Roger of Wendover*, Vol. II., *Annal 1204*. Bohn's Libraries. G. Bell & Sons.

Thus the castle of the Rock of Andelys fell into the hands of the French King on the 6th of March, and Roger de Lacy with all his followers were taken to France, where, on account of the bravery he had shown in defence of his castle, he was detained prisoner on parole. On this all the holders of castles in the transmarine territories, with the citizens and other subjects of the King of England, sent messages to England to tell him in what a precarious situation they were placed, and that the time, according to the terms of the treaty, was near, when they must either give up the cities and castles to the King of the French, or consign to destruction the hostages which they had given him. To which message King John answered, and intimated by the same messengers to all of them, that they were to expect no assistance from him, but that they each were to do what seemed best to him. And thus, all kind of defence failing in those provinces, the whole of Normandy, Tours, Anjou, and Poictou, with the cities, castles, and other possessions, except the Castles of Rochelle, Thouars, and Niorz, fell to the dominion of the King of the French. When this was told to the English King, he was enjoying all the pleasures of life with his Queen, in whose company he believed that he possessed everything he wanted; moreover, he felt confidence in the immensity of the wealth he had collected, as if by that he could regain the territory he had lost.

LONDON (CIRC. 1204).

Richard of Devizes

Source.—*Richard of Devizes, Chronicles of the Crusades*, § 80. Bohn's Libraries. G. Bell & Sons.

Every race of men, out of every nation which is under heaven, resort thither in great numbers; every nation has introduced into that city its vices and bad manners. No one lives in it without offence; there is not a single street in it that does not abound in miserable, obscene wretches; there, in proportion as any man has exceeded in wickedness, so much is he the better. I am not ignorant of the disposition I am exhorting; you have, in addition to your youth, an ardent disposition, a slowness of memory and a soberness of reason between extremes. I feel in myself no uneasiness about you, unless you should abide with men of corrupt lives; for from our associations our manners are formed. But let that be as it may. You will come to London. Behold! I warn you, whatever of evil or perversity there is in any, whatever in all parts of the world, you will find in that city alone. Go not to the dances of panders, nor mix yourself up with the herds of the houses of ill fame; avoid the talus and the dice, the theatre and the tavern. You will find more braggadocios there than in all France, while the number of flatterers is infinite. Stage-players, buffoons, those that have no hair on their bodies, Garamantes, pick-thanks, catamites, effeminate evildoers, lewd musical girls, druggists, lustful persons, fortune-tellers, extortioners, nightly strollers, magicians, mimics, common beggars, tatterdemalions—this whole crew has filled every house. So if you do not wish to live with the shameful, you will not dwell in London.

THE TOWNS OF ENGLAND. CIRC. 1190-1206.

Richard of Devizes

I am not speaking against the learned, whether monks or Jews; although, still, from their very dwelling together with such evil persons, I should esteem them less perfect there than elsewhere.

Nor does my advice go so far, as that you should betake yourself to no city; with my counsel you will take up your residence nowhere but in a town, though it remains to say in what.

Therefore, if you should land near Canterbury, you will have to lose your way, if even you should but pass through it. It is an assemblage of the vilest, entirely devoted to their—I know not whom, but who has been lately canonized, and had been the Archbishop of Canterbury, as everywhere they die in the open day in the streets for want of bread and employment.

Rochester and Chichester are mere villages, and they possess nothing for which they should be called cities, but the Sees of their bishops. Oxford scarcely, I will not say satisfies, but sustains its clerks. Exeter supports men and beasts with the same grain. Bath is placed, or rather buried, in the lowest parts of the valleys, in a very dense atmosphere and sulphury vapour, as it were at the gates of Hell. Nor yet will you select your habitation in the Northern cities nor in Worcester, Chester, Hereford, on account of the desperate Welshmen. York abounds in Scots, vile and faithless men, or rather rascals. The town of Ely is always putrefied by the surrounding marshes. In Durham, Norwich, or Lincoln, there are very few of your disposition among the powerful; you will never hear anyone speak French. At Bristol there is nobody who is not, or has not been, a soap-maker, and every Frenchman esteems soap-makers as he does nightmen.

After the cities, every market, village or town, has but rude and rustic inhabitants. Moreover, at all times, account the Cornish people for such as you know our Flemish are accounted in France. For the rest, the kingdom itself is generally most favoured with the dew of heaven and the fatness of the earth; and in every place there are some good, but much fewer in them all than in Winchester alone.

This is in those parts the Jerusalem of the Jews, in it alone they enjoy perpetual peace; it is the school of those who desire to live well and prosper. Here they become men, here there is bread and wine enough for nothing. There are therein monks of such compassion and gentleness, clergy of such understanding and frankness, citizens of such civility and good faith, ladies of such beauty and modesty, that little hinders but I should go there and become a Christian with such Christians. To that city I direct you, the city of cities, the mother of all, the best above all.

There is but one fault, and that alone in which they customarily indulge too much. With the exception I should say of the learned and of the Jews, the Winchester people tell lies like watchmen, but it is in making up reports. For in no place under heaven so many false rumours are fabricated so easily as there; otherwise they are true in everything.

JOHN'S GRANT TO THE ABBEY OF CROYLAND (1202-1206).

Ingulph's "Chronicles"

Source. — *Ingulph's Chronicles.* Bohn's Libraries. G. Bell & Sons.

The Charter of our lord the King, John, as to the confirmation of the boundaries of the abbey, and of which mention is made above, was to the following effect: "John, by the Grace of God, King of England, lord of Ireland, duke of Normandy and Aquitaine, and Earl of Anjou, to the archbishops, bishops, abbots, earls, barons, justiciaries, sheriffs, and all his bailiffs and faithful subjects, greeting. Know ye, that we have granted and confirmed unto God and the Church of St. Guthlac at Croyland, and to the abbot and monks there serving God, all the lands and tenements, and other the possessions to the said church belonging, and in especial the site of the said abbey, together with the boundaries thereof herein named, which extend as follow: a distance of five leagues, from Croyland to the place where the Asendyk falls into the waters of the Welland, together with all piscaries to the said boundaries belonging. Wherefore we do will and strictly command that the before-named church, and abbot, and monks shall hold and for ever possess all their lands, tenements, and other their possessions, and all the gifts which since the death of King Henry, the grandfather of our father, have been reasonably given to them, fully, peacefully, freely, quietly, and honourably, to enjoy the same in wood and in plain, in meadows and in pastures, in waters and in marshes, in preserves and in fisheries, in mills and in mill-dams, and in all other things and places, with right of Sach and Soch, and Thol, and Them, and Infangthefe, and with all other free customs and acquittances, as fully, freely, and quietly as the said church, and abbot, and monks, held the same in the time of King Henry, the grandfather of our father, or other our predecessors Kings of England, and as fully, freely, and quietly as any churches in our kingdom of England hold the same, in such manner as is by the Charter of King Henry our father reasonably testified, etc. Given by the hand of Simon, Archdeacon of Wells."

Not even thus, however, did the venerable abbot Henry gain the wish for repose, but, like a stone out of the living rock to be placed in a heavenly house, was he squared, both on the right side and on the left, by repeated blows and numerous buffetings. For Acharius, also the Abbot of Burgh St. Peter (not content with his own boundaries, but desirous, contrary to the prophetic warning "to join house to house, and lay field to field, till there be no place,") first, by the royal writ, obtained of the King from beyond sea, impleaded the said abbot Henry, and without any good reason claimed against him our southern marsh called Alderland, of which our monastery had held undisturbed possession from its foundation until the times of our said father, just as the Assyrians did against the people of God. Upon this, Hubert, Archbishop of Canterbury, who was then chief justiciary of England, sent letters mandatory to the abbats of Ramsay and Thorney, directing them to make inquisition in his behalf upon the oaths of eighteen knights, mutually agreed upon, what right each of them had to the lands, meadows, pastures, and marshes, and all other things between the river Rene, and the river Welland, and which ought to be the boundaries between the Abbey of Burgh and the Abbey of Croyland, and fully to state the said inquisition, under their seals, and those of the knights to the before-named archbishop and justices.

A dissension, however, arising between the inquisitors, they returned to their homes, leaving the matter unsettled.

At length, however, after many conferences, discussions, delays, and expenses on both sides the dispute between the two abbats having been enquired into at great length before the justices of our lord the King at Lexington, was finally settled to the no small detriment of the church of Croyland.

THE ELECTION OF LANGTON (1207).

Roger of Wendover

Source.—*Roger of Wendover*, Vol. II., *Annal 1207*. Bohn's Libraries. G. Bell & Sons.

About this time the monks of the church of Canterbury appeared before our lord the Pope, to plead a disgraceful dispute which had arisen between themselves; for a certain part of them, by authenticated letters of the convent, presented Reginald, sub-prior of Canterbury, as they had often done, to be archbishop-elect, and earnestly required the confirmation of his election; the other portion of the same monks had, by letters alike authentic, presented John, bishop of Norwich, showing by many arguments that the election of the sub-prior was null, not only because it had been made by night, and without the usual ceremonies, and without the consent of the King, but also because it had not been made by the older and wiser part of the convent; and thus setting forth these reasons, they asked that that election should be confirmed, which was made before fitting witnesses in open day and by consent, and in the presence of the King. At length, after long arguments on both sides, our lord the Pope, seeing that the parties could not agree in fixing on the same person, and that both elections had been made irregularly, and not according to the decrees of the holy canons, by the advice of his cardinals, annulled both elections, laying the apostolic interdict on the parties, and by definitive judgment ordering, that neither of them should again aspire to the honours of the archbishopric. When at length the letters of our lord the Pope came to the notice of the English King, he was exceedingly enraged, as much at the promotion of Stephen Langton, as at the annulling of the election of the bishop of Norwich, and accused the monks of Canterbury of treachery; for he said that they had, to the prejudice of his rights, elected their sub-prior without his permission, and afterwards, to palliate their fault by giving satisfaction to him, they chose the bishop of Norwich; that they had also received money from the treasury for their expenses in obtaining the confirmation of the said bishop's election from the apostolic see; and to complete their iniquity, they had there elected Stephen Langton, his open enemy, and had obtained his consecration to the archbishopric. On this account the said King, in the fury of his anger and indignation, sent Fulk de Cantelu and Henry de Cornhill, two most cruel and inhuman knights, with armed attendants, to expel the monks of Canterbury, as if they were guilty of a crime against his injured majesty from England, or else to consign them to capital punishment. These knights were not slow to obey the commands of their lord, but set out for Canterbury, and, entering the monastery with drawn swords, in the King's name fiercely ordered the prior and monks to depart immediately from the kingdom of England as traitors to the King's Majesty; and they affirmed with an oath that, if they (the monks) refused to do this, they would themselves set fire to the monastery, and the other offices adjoining it, and would burn all the monks themselves with their buildings. The monks, acting unadvisedly, departed without violence or laying hands on anyone; all of them, except thirteen sick men who were lying in the infirmary unable to walk, forthwith crossed into Flanders, and were honourably received at the Abbey of St. Bertinus and other monasteries on the Continent. Afterwards, by the orders of the King, some monks of the order of St. Augustine were placed in the church of Canterbury in their stead to perform the duties there; the before-mentioned bulk managing, and even distributing and confiscating, all the property of the same monks, whilst their lands and those of the archbishop remained uncultivated. The aforesaid monks were driven from their monastery into exile on the fourteenth of July.

THE INTERDICT (1208).

Roger of Wendover

Source. — *Roger of Wendover*, Vol. II., *Annal 1208*. Bohn's Libraries. G. Bell & Sons.

The Bishops of London, Ely, and Winchester, in execution of the legateship entrusted to them, went to King John, and after duly setting forth the apostolic commands, entreated of him humbly and with tears, that he, having God in his sight, would recall the archbishop and the monks of Canterbury to their Church, and honour and love them with perfect affection, and they informed him that thus he would avoid the shame of an interdict, and the Disposer of rewards, would if he did so, multiply his temporal honours on him, and after his death would bestow lasting glory on him. When the said bishops wished, out of regard to the King, to prolong the discourse, the King became nearly mad with rage, and broke forth in words of blasphemy against the Pope and his cardinals, swearing by God's teeth, that, if they or any other priests soever presumptuously dared to lay his dominions under an interdict, he would immediately send all the prelates of England, clerks as well as ordained persons, to the Pope, and confiscate all their property; he added, moreover, that all the clerks of Rome or of the Pope himself who could be found in England or in his other territories, he would send to Rome with their eyes plucked out, and their noses slit, that by these marks they might be known there from other people; in addition to this, he plainly ordered the bishops to take themselves quickly from his sight if they wished to keep their bodies free from harm.

THE BATTLE OF BOUVINES (1214).

Matthew of Westminster

Source.—*Matthew of Westminster*, Vol. II., p. 119. Bohn's Libraries. G. Bell & Sons.

The Count of Flanders and William, Earl of Salisbury, by making a prodigal distribution of the King's treasures, collected a numerous army of hired mercenaries, having formed a design of suddenly attacking Philip, King of France on a Sunday, as he was not accustomed to bear arms on that day. They had also great hope from, and great reliance in, the wisdom and assistance of the Emperor Otho, who was, as it were, watching for a struggle with a drawn sword.

Accordingly the battle of Bouvines in Flanders was fought, and great bravery was shown on both sides. The King of France had three fine horses stabbed under him, nevertheless by the assistance of God he that day gained an important triumph over his enemies. Many nobles both of the Empire and of the kingdom of England were taken prisoners, but the Emperor escaped with a few of his men who were at hand. To the greater confusion of King John, he was repulsed from the castle which is called Monk's Rock, in consequence of the arrival of Louis, a son of the King of France; so that hearing the news of the taking of his nobles at Bouvines, he felt both God and man were offended with, and hostile to him. Accordingly he fled disgracefully and ignominiously from the siege before mentioned, and if he had not given eleven thousand marks of silver for a truce for 3 years and then retreated into England with all speed, he would no doubt have been taken, to his great disgrace.

EVENTS LEADING TO THE MAGNA CHARTA (1214).

Roger of Wendover

Source.—*Roger of Wendover*, Vol. II., *Annal 1214*. Bohn's Libraries. G. Bell & Sons.

On the 25th of August in the same year, Stephen, Archbishop of Canterbury, with the bishops, abbots, priors, deacons, and barons of the kingdom assembled at St. Paul's in the City of London, and there the archbishop granted permission to the Conventual Churches, as well as to the secular priests, to chant the services of the church in a low voice, in the hearing of their parishioners. At this conference, as report asserts, the said archbishop called some of the nobles aside to him, and conversed privately with them to the following effect: "Did you hear," said he, "how, when I absolved the King at Winchester, I made him swear that he would do away with unjust laws, and would recall good laws, such as those of King Edward, and cause them to be observed by all in the kingdom; a Charter of Henry Ist of England has just now been found, by which you may, if you wish it, recall your long-lost rights and your former condition."

*   *   *   *   *

On the Monday next after the octaves of Easter, the said barons assembled in the town of Brackley, and when the King learned this, he sent the archbishop of Canterbury, and William Marshal earl of Pembroke, with some other prudent men, to them to enquire what the laws and liberties were which they demanded. The barons then delivered to the messengers a paper, containing in great measure the laws and ancient customs of the kingdom, and declared that, unless the King immediately granted them and confirmed them under his own seal, they would, by taking possession of his fortresses, force him to give them sufficient satisfaction as to their before-named demands. The archbishop with his fellow messengers then carried the paper to the King, and read to him the heads of the paper one by one throughout.

The King when he heard the purport of these heads, derisively said, with the greatest indignation, "Why, amongst these unjust demands, did not the barons ask for my kingdom also? Their demands are vain and visionary, and are unsupported by any plea of reason whatever." And at length he angrily declared with an oath, that he would never grant them such liberties as would render him their slave. The principal of these laws and liberties, which the nobles required to be confirmed to them, are partly described above in the Charter of King Henry, and partly extracted from the old laws of King Edward as the following history will show in due time.

KING JOHN AND THE ABBOT
OF CANTERBURY.

Traditional Ballad of the 13th Century

[Traditional ballad of the 13th century. Probably of Coptic folk-lore and transferred to John. Thus it illustrates the reputation of John and not an actual incident.]

An ancient story I'll tell you anon
Of a notable prince that was called King John;
And he ruled England with main and with might,
For he did great wrong and maintain'd little right.

And I'll tell you a story, a story so merry
Concerning the Abbot of Canterbury;
How for his house-keeping, and high renown,
They rode post for him to London town.

An hundred men the King did hearsay,
The Abbot kept in his house every day;
And fifty gold chains, without any doubt,
In velvet coats waited the Abbot about.

"How now, father Abbot, I hear it of thee,
Thou keepest a far better house than me,
And for thy house-keeping, and high renown,
I fear thou work'st treason against my crown."

"My liege," quo' the Abbot, "I would it were known,
I never spend nothing but what is my own;
And I trust, your grace will do me no dere,
For spending of my own true-gotten gere."

"Yes, yes, father Abbot, thy fault it is high,
And now for the same thou needest must die;
For except thou canst answer me questions three,
Thy head shall be smitten from thy body.

"And first," quo' the King, "When I'm in this stead,
With my crown of gold so fair on my head;
Among all my liege-men so noble of birth
Thou must tell me to one penny what I am worth.

"Secondly, tell me, without any doubt,

How soon I may ride the whole world about;
And at the third question thou must no shrink,
But tell me here truly, what I do think."

"O, these are hard questions for my shallow wit,
Nor I cannot answer your grace as yet;
But if you will give me but three weeks' space,
I'll do my endeavour to answer your grace."

"Now three weeks' space to thee I will give,
And that is the longest time thou hast to live;
For if thou dost not answer my questions three,
Thy lands and thy livings are forfeit to me."

Away rode the Abbot all sad at that word,
And he rode to Cambridge and Oxenford;
But never a doctor there was so wise,
That could with his learning an answer devize.

Then home rode the Abbot of comfort so cold,
And he met his shepherd a going to fold:
"How now, my lord Abbot, you are welcome home;
What news do you bring us from good King John?"

"Sad news, sad news, shepherd, I must give;
That I have but three days more to live:
For if I do not answer him questions three,
My head will be smitten from my body.

"The first is to tell him there in that stead
With his crown of gold so fair on his head,
Among all his liege-men so noble of birth,
To within one penny of what he is worth.

"The second, to tell him, without any doubt,
How soon he may ride this whole world about:
And at the third question I must not shrink,
But tell him there truly what he does think."

"Now cheer up, sir Abbot, did you never hear yet,
That a fool he may learn a wise man to wit?
Lend one horse, and serving men, and your apparel,
And I'll ride to London to answer your quarrel.

"Nay, frown not, if it hath been told unto me,
I am like your lordship as ever may be;
And if you will but lend me your gown,
There is none shall know us at fair London town."

"Now horses, and serving men thou shalt have,
With sumptuous array most gallant and brave;
With crozier, and mitre, and rochet, and cope,
Fit to appear 'fore our father the Pope."

"Now welcome Sir Abbot," the King he did say,
"'Tis well thou'rt come back to keep thy day;
For an if thou canst answer my questions three,
Thy life and thy living both savéd shall be.

"And first, when thou seest here in this stead,
With my crown of gold so fair on my head,
Among all my liege-men so noble of birth,
Tell me to one penny what I am worth."

"For thirty pence our Saviour was sold
Among the false Jews, as I have been told;
And twenty-nine is the worth of thee,
For I think thou art one penny worser than he."

The King he laughed and swore by St. Bittel
"I did not think I had been worth so little!
—Now secondly tell me, without any doubt,
How soon I may ride this whole world about."

"You must rise with the sun, and ride with the same,
Until the next morning he riseth again;
And then your grace need not make any doubt,
But in twenty-four hours you'll ride it about."

The King he laughed and swore by St. John,
"I did not think it could be gone so soon!
—Now from the third question thou must not shrink,
But tell me here truly what I do think."

"Yea, that I shall do, and make your grace merry:
You think I'm the Abbot of Canterbury;
But I'm his poor shepherd, as plain you may see,
That am come to beg pardon for him and for me."

The King he laughed and swore by the mass,
"I'll make thee lord abbot this day in his place!"
"Now, nay, my liege, be not in such speed,
For alack, I can neither write, nor read."

"Four nobles a week, then, I will give thee,
For this merry jest thou hast shown unto me;
And tell the old Abbot when thou comest home,
Thou has brought him a pardon from good King John."

THE LAST DAYS OF KING JOHN (1216).

Matthew of Westminster

Source.—*Matthew of Westminster*, Vol. II., pp. 127, 128. G. Bell & Sons.

Prince Louis and all his followers embarked on board the ships, and came with a fair wind to the isle of Thanet, and anchored in the place which is called Stanhore, on the 21st of May. King John was at that time with his army at Dover, but as he was surrounded by a band of foreign mercenaries, who loved Louis more than John, King of England, he did not dare to encounter Louis in a hostile manner, lest his troups might perchance desert King John himself in his necessity, and transfer themselves to Louis. From which considerations he preferred retreating at the time to engaging in a doubtful battle. Therefore, he retreated, and withdrew to Canterbury, and left and entrusted the Castle of Dover to the custody and good faith of Hubert de Burgh. And soon afterwards, Gualo, the legate, landed in England, for the protection of King John and the kingdom against Louis and his partisans. But King John fled as far as Winchester, and Louis, when he found that no one offered to resist him, disembarked from his ships, and landing at Sandwich, subdued immediately the whole of that district, with the exception of the town of Dover, and hastening towards London, he made himself master of the Castle of Rochester, and on the 2nd of June he arrived in London, where first of all he offered up prayers at St. Paul's, and was afterwards publicly received by the clergy and laity with great joy, and received the fealty and homage of all the barons. And shortly afterwards, namely on the 14th of June, the city of Winchester was surrendered to him; and on the day after the feast of Saint John, he took the castle of the city, and the bishop's castle also; and on the 9th of July he received the submission of the Castles of Odiham, Farnham, Guildford and Reigate. The Castle of Windsor was besieged by the earls and barons of both France and England, but they were forced to retreat from before it, without succeeding in their object. But the Castle of Cambridge was taken by the barons, with twenty esquires which were found in it.

The same year Gualo, the legate, exacted visitation fees throughout all England, from all the cathedral churches and houses of religious brotherhoods, fixing each visitation fee at fifty shillings. He also seized all the benefices of the clergy and men of religious orders, who adhered to Louis and the barons, and converted them to the use of his own clergy. In the meantime, King John, inflamed with the madness of passion, oppressed and grievously afflicted the provinces of Suffolk and Norfolk. Then, continuing his march towards the north, he irrecoverably lost his carriages, and much of his baggage at Wellester, where they were swallowed up by a quicksand. And when he heard the news he grieved inconsolably, and redoubling deep sighs, he passed the night at Swineshead Abbey, belonging to the Carthusian order, where according to his custom, he gorged himself with peaches soaked in new wine and cider, and being greatly absorbed in grief for his recent loss, he became attacked with a severe illness.

But the next day, concealing his illness lest the enemy should triumph over him, he, though with difficulty, mounted his horse; and soon afterwards, having had a litter drawn by horses made for him, he dismounted from his palfrey and entered it, and in this way he came to the Castle of Leadford, where he spent the night, and found his disease increase greatly. But the next day he was carried forwards and arrived at the Castle of Newark where he took to his bed, and his sickness assumed a fatal appearance; and summoning the Abbot of Crofestune, who was skilful in the art of medicine, to his side, he confessed himself to him, and received the eucharist from him. And he appointed Henry, his eldest son, the heir of his kingdom, bequeathing his body to the Church of Worcester, under the protection of Saint Wolstan. After this, with the greatest bitterness of spirit, he cursed all his barons, instead of bidding them farewell; and in this manner, poor, deprived of all his treasures, and not retaining the smallest portion of land in peace, so that he was truly called Lackland, he most miserably departed from this life on the night following the next after the day of Saint Luke the Evangelist. And because this John made himself detestable to many persons, not only on account of the death of his nephew, Arthur, but also on account of his tyrannical conduct, and of the tribute with which he bound the kingdom of England under perpetual slavery, and of the war which his misdeeds provoked, he scarcely deserved to be mourned by the lamentations of any one.

The following are the territories which John lost by his cruelties and oppressions, which he did not resist from doing to everyone. First of all the duchy of Normandy, the County of Blois, the County of Maine, Anjou, Poitou, the Limosin, Auvergne and Angoulême. And all these districts at one time belonged to King John. Besides this he subjected England and Ireland to the payment of tribute, and never recovered any of his losses, to the day of his death.

Lector House believes that a society develops through a two-fold approach of continuous learning and adaptation, which is derived from the study of classic literary works spread across the historic timeline of literature records. Therefore, we aim at reviving, repairing and redeveloping all those inaccessible or damaged but historically as well as culturally important literature across subjects so that the future generations may have an opportunity to study and learn from past works to embark upon a journey of creating a better future.

This book is a result of an effort made by Lector House towards making a contribution to the preservation and repair of original ancient works which might hold historical significance to the approach of continuous learning across subjects.

HAPPY READING & LEARNING!

LECTOR HOUSE LLP
E-MAIL: lectorpublishing@gmail.com